Miss Jessie's®

Miss Jessie's®

CREATING A SUCCESSFUL BUSINESS
FROM SCRATCH—NATURALLY

★ ★ ★ ★ ★

MIKO BRANCH

Amistad

An Imprint of HarperCollins*Publishers*

MISS JESSIE'S Copyright © 2015 by Miko Branch. All rights reserved. Printed in the United States of America. No part of this book may be used or reproduced in any manner whatsoever without written permission except in the case of brief quotations embodied in critical articles and reviews. For information, address HarperCollins Publishers, 195 Broadway, New York, NY 10007.

HarperCollins books may be purchased for educational, business, or sales promotional use. For information, please e-mail the Special Markets Department at SPsales@harpercollins.com.

FIRST EDITION

Designed by Suet Yee Chong

Library of Congress Cataloging-in-Publication Data has been applied for.

ISBN: 978-0-06-232918-9

15 16 17 18 19   OV/RRD   10 9 8 7 6 5 4 3 2

To Titi Cree Branch, my beloved sister:
may your legacy live forever.

★ ★ ★

CONTENTS

★ ★ ★

PREFACE
STORIES AND RECIPES FROM OUR KITCHEN TABLE
xi

ONE
MAKING SOMETHING OUT OF NOTHING
1

TWO
DEEP ROOTS
9

THREE
STREET WISE
45

FOUR
YOUNG, GIFTED, AND BLACK-OWNED
67

FIVE
READY TO ROLL
83

SIX
HARD PRESSED
101

SEVEN
IT'S ALL ABOUT THE HAIR
121

EIGHT
THE BEST DAMN CURL CRÈME, PERIOD!
155

NINE
A SUDDEN TWIST
191

TEN
TRANSITIONERS
203

ELEVEN
BULL'S-EYE
221

TWELVE
NEW GROWTH
233

THIRTEEN
BIG ROLLERS
253

EPILOGUE   271

LETTER TO TITI   275
ACKNOWLEDGMENTS   279
GLOSSARY OF RETAIL TERMS   283
THE LANGUAGE OF HAIR: DEFINITIONS   287
PRODUCT DEFINITIONS   289

PREFACE

Stories and Recipes from Our Kitchen Table

Saturday mornings are sacred to me. It's when I work in our hair salon in Manhattan's SoHo and am up close and personal with Miss Jessie's most loyal customers. I'm always eager to hear their latest news about what's going on in their lives. Not only is it my chance to catch up with old friends, it's an opportunity to touch and feel what's going on with their hair. I consider myself their collaborator as they develop their naturally curly looks, and I love to see the progress we're making.

I make a point of getting to the salon on Broadway bright and early to prepare for the dozen or more women who I know will be coming in that morning to get their curls treated and styled. We pride ourselves on working fast, getting everyone in and out the door within a reasonable amount of time. My small team of stylists and I run our washing and styling stations with clocklike precision, each of us flitting from one head to the next, massaging in our styling treatments to elongate the curls, blowing the hair straight, cutting, and then manipulating their tresses to bring out their best curls. While we work, we talk to our customers about their hair issues and recommend products and techniques, often in the context of whatever is going on in their lives, whether they're dating, having babies, or simply trying to find the right wash-n-go style to suit their busy work schedules. The atmosphere is bright and the conversation is flowing. Although we are working, it never feels like work. Best of all, I get to see the joy in the faces of these women as they watch their hair transformation. Watching them discover and embrace the beauty of their God-given hair texture is something that never gets old.

Whether it's through the salon business, or through our line of Miss Jessie's curly-hair-care products, my sister, Titi, and I have had the privilege of being part of a revolution in naturally curly hair since the 1990s. As co-owners of Miss Jessie's, we've helped transform an industry as well as a culture, changing the way women around the globe embrace their natural hair texture. This is the story of how we did it and a blueprint for how you, too, can become an entrepreneur and make waves in any industry you choose.

Over the years, we have built several businesses: a family cleaning business with our father; an underground mom-and-pop business consisting of a single-chair home salon; our Bond and Hancock Street salons; Curve \ Miss Jessie's salon, our e-commerce business; and our mass retail operation. Along the way we learned and relearned many lessons that you can apply as a small-business proprietor and an ambitious entrepreneur.

One of the first takeaways is that you don't need money to transform an industry. You don't even need privileges or contacts. My sister and I did not train or go to school to build a multimillion-dollar company from scratch. We don't have MBAs, and we didn't get bank loans or find angel investors. What we had was the seed of an idea, an entrepreneurial fire in our bellies, and a solid foundation of family and influences to learn from and observe, lending us the common sense, resourcefulness, and work ethic necessary to follow through on that dream.

That's the story we want to share in this book. There's a message here for every individual who doesn't feel that he or she has an opportunity to be successful, whether that person is young, a single mother, working-class and coming up without advantages, or an aspiring hairdresser who wants to dream big. We did it; so can you.

To understand the DNA of our company and how we came to be the multimillion-dollar enterprise we are today, it's necessary to know where we come from and the unconventional way we were raised. Miss Jessie's is not just a business, it is deeply personal, and everything—from how we do hair to the choices we make in building the company—is inextricably linked to who we are as individuals. This business is so much more than a moneymaking enterprise: It is the authentic reflection of everything we stand for.

It all started with family and the way we were raised. Our upbringing and the generations of our family who worked hard and created something from nothing are among the key ingredients in our story. Who we are today and all we have built are based on a lifetime's worth of learning that began from the time we could crawl. Titi and I absorbed everything we could from our unconventional upbringing, taking from our Japanese mother's Zen aesthetic and our black father's steely determination that we make something of ourselves, and the homespun grace of our Southern-belle grandmother, Miss Jessie: our company's namesake and one of the strongest and most resourceful women we have ever met.

Over these next pages, you will meet the friends, family members, and mentors who were a part of our journey, many of whom remain connected to our business. You will learn how we soaked up the entrepreneurial and creative culture of the early hip-hop era on the streets of Queens, in Brooklyn's artistic and business-minded mecca in the late nineties, and in the high-end salons of Manhattan. Before we made any kind of money or enjoyed any kind of business success, we put that knowledge to the test, picking up and absorbing all we could. We sampled everything, distilling and filing away what worked for us.

No single influence took over, and this enabled us to see a trend, find out what worked, and take it to a whole new level. It played out particularly in the way we leveraged the movement toward naturally curly hair, keeping our distance by showing, rather than telling, millions of women how they could have beautiful, healthy hair whatever their hair texture or ethnicity. And through redefining this movement, we empowered countless women by helping them transform the way they felt not just about their naturally curly hair but about themselves.

There is a long, rich, and complex history surrounding African-American women's hair that ties to views on self-image. For generations, many black women were made to feel inferior as they faced the constant pressure to conform to European standards of beauty. This resulted in a kind of backlash, with a small but growing population of women forgoing harsh relaxers, weaves, and wigs. Grooming options for the "natural" market had long been limited to Afros, dreadlocks, and braids—looks that have not yet gained full acceptance in mainstream and corporate environments.

We learned a lot from the examples of those who came before us. When my sister and I decided that we were going to go into the business of curly hair, our father, in typical fashion, handed us a book, *On Her Own Ground,* a biography of legendary entrepreneur and philanthropist Madam C. J. Walker, brilliantly written by her great-great-granddaughter A'Lelia Bundles. "Read this," he said. "You could learn a lot from a great woman like her." He was right. Entirely on her own and with no resources to speak of, she created hair products and launched an industry where none existed before.

Standing on her shoulders, we made it our mission to develop hair services and products that allow today's women to have natural hair that is manageable, well groomed, and glamorous. Yes, the hair you were born with is a blessing, and we will prove it with plenty of before-and-after pictures. We will show you, just like we have demonstrated to our customers time and again, that it is possible to have the best of both worlds.

Of course, the naturally-curly-hair movement is just one of the many gorgeous strands that make up the story of *Miss Jessie's.* This is also a tale of the evolution of our business and brand from the kitchen table of our brownstone in Brooklyn to the shelves of major retailers around the globe. Along the way, we'll share the origins of the curly-hair revolution. Before we developed the product line, there were very few solutions in the market that existed for women with curly hair, particularly African-Americans. But as Miss Jessie's caught fire, building a cult following and establishing a completely new product category in national chains like Target and CVS, recognition of the huge market potential grew, and corporate America joined the stampede to cater to a more ethnically diverse consumer.

This competition is validation for all that we've accomplished by staying true to who we are and never compromising on quality. We're proud to say that Miss Jessie's holds the lead, with a growing range of premium products based on intimate knowledge of the customers we serve. We know our customers like no one else because we *are* our own best customers, enabling us to offer women of various ethnicities beautiful solutions.

Miss Jessie's is also the story of how our sister act reinvented the rules and followed instincts to become industry leaders. This book, which is both a memoir and a business how-to, details our hard-won lessons surviving as cheap labor for our father's latest enterprise; being left to lean on ourselves as latchkey kids in Jamaica, Queens; learning about creating something from nothing at the kitchen table of our ever resourceful and inspiring grandmother, Miss Jessie; and blossoming as independent young women with bills to pay and dreams to build. It talks about the evolution of Miss Jessie's from a single salon chair in a Brooklyn loft living room to a global product company that regularly graces the pages of *Lucky, Glamour, Essence, Allure,* and *O* magazines, laying out the highs and lows of a family partnership with intense candor and realism.

Above all, *Miss Jessie's* is about the building of a business and a brand, with specific takeaways on how to do the same thing successfully in any industry. Miss Jessie's is part of the backbone of the American economy—a Main Street business that expands and hires, creating jobs and prosperity. This book imparts advice and wisdom that is rooted in the real-life experience of developing a business within a recessionary economy.

Through our own example, and the stories of those who have inspired us, we will guide you through the process of building your own business. You'll learn how, after soaking up a myriad of influences in your earliest years, it's possible to find your own lane and turn your unique experiences into a revenue stream. Once you have your idea and a passion to see it through, you will find, with the help of our book, that it's possible to create something from nothing—no excuses.

Throughout, you will gain valuable, actionable insights for your own business, like knowing your worth and pricing accordingly, and applying careful financial management that enables you to survive challenges. You will learn that employing grassroots word-of-mouth marketing revenues can build a core customer base; that engaging in a dialogue with the customer is an effective form of research and development; and that taking a precise and cautious approach to business expansion is essential to protect all that you have worked hard to build.

These were some of the many life and business lessons that launched us on our trajectory, turning our dream of becoming independent, self-sufficient entrepreneurs into an even bigger reality as we became the owners of a global hair-care brand. Our path to success was by no means conventional. We did not go to business school, and we had no family connections or money to speak of. But we had the raw ingredients of ingenuity, ambition, street smarts, and hard work. Into that mixture we added our experiences, along with the wisdom of our father, our mother, and our beloved grandmother, Miss Jessie. Binding it all together were the love and devotion we had for each other as sisters. That is how we created our business from scratch—naturally.

Miss Jessie's ®

★ ★ ★

One

MAKING SOMETHING OUT OF NOTHING

What is excellent is always beautiful.

—KERRY JAMES MARSHALL

Miko, Miko, wake up! I've cracked the nut!"
    Those were the words shouted by my sister, startling me out of a deep sleep. As I blinked a few times, slowly taking in the harsh light, she came into focus. Her beaming face said it all. Not one prone to exaggeration, Titi was a serious woman and did not excite easily or without cause. I knew that this was an important moment. After months of our experimentation, using our Brooklyn brownstone kitchen as a test lab, Titi had every right to wake me up to celebrate. Standing over my bed, she was holding up a version of the hairstyling cream that

we had been trying for many months to get just right. As she swirled the mixture around and rubbed it between her thumb and index fingers, holding it up to my nose for a sniff, I could tell that everything about it was perfect.

The smell took me right back to the warm kitchen of Miss Jessie, our grandmother.

"MIKO, GO GET ME THAT POT!" ordered Miss Jessie from the central command post of her kitchen table. "No, not that one. The one with the black handle, to the left!" she corrected, peering up at me while never missing a beat at her chopping board as she cut onions and celery into fine, even pieces. "Titi, ain't you done peeling them potatoes yet?" Miss Jessie raised her voice, this time at my sister. "C'mon now, we can't keep waiting on you. You know I got to get my turkey in the oven, and then make my pies, too."

Making that potato salad was like a military operation. Any stray grandchild who wandered into her kitchen was put to work, fetching, peeling, and mixing to help her produce the most delicious meals, made with love, experience, and an unerring sense of what worked. This was where the magic happened. Our paternal grandmother's house in Poughkeepsie, New York, was the center of our lives, and her kitchen table was where Titi and I absorbed our greatest life lessons. It was the place where we were fed the incredible food and wisdom that would nourish and sustain us well into adulthood.

One of those lessons was how to make the best product possible, whether it was potato salad, sweet potato pie, or yellow cake batter. Miss Jessie never compromised. Her ingredients had to be the best. She used to go shopping every weekend at a local farmer's market called Adam's; that hapless store manager must have braced himself whenever he saw her coming. Miss Jessie used to inspect the potatoes as if they were fine diamonds, scrutinizing each flaw. For her salad, each one had to look good, with as few brown spots as possible. They had to be fresh, just dug up from the soil, and with her keen sense of smell, she could always tell. They also had to be the right color, weight, and consistency. She preferred the waxy yellow kind from Idaho, which held up best to boiling and mixing and had the most flavor. But she wasn't going to pay top dollar for them. Heck, no! Watching Miss Jessie bargain the store staff down on price made us wish we had her in Washington, working on the next international trade deal or peace treaty. She was that good.

Once she got her ingredients home, chopped, and prepared, it was all about the mixing. For the potato salad, she always used the same large ceramic bowl. But she never relied on mixing utensils. Everything had to be gently and thoroughly blended by hand, to ensure that every morsel got coated with the mayonnaise she made from scratch. Then she fine-tuned, adding eggs for body, vinegar and sugar to bring out the zest, a dash of paprika for color, and delicately cut pieces of red bell pepper for a pretty garnish.

When it was all done, and the meal had been served and enjoyed by the family members gathered at her house that Sunday, Miss Jessie would package the leftovers in her best Tupperware. Each container had to be the same size and color, so that we could each go home with an equal portion of food. It was usually enough to last us the rest of the week, enough that we could share it with the aunts, uncles, and cousins who'd missed out.

Whatever Miss Jessie was making, whether it was potato salad, peach cobbler, macaroni and cheese, or a frosted vanilla cake, had to be perfection. Each ingredient had to be properly sourced, and only the freshest and most flavorful would do. Our grandmother never stinted on quality, although she was never a fool on price. We took that same approach when we sourced our materials for business.

She was also a stickler for presentation. Whatever came out of her kitchen had to look, smell, and taste heavenly. The texture and color had to be just right. Her food was an experience for all the senses. Titi and I would later apply all of this knowledge and experience to our own products, putting the same love and care into our line of styling creams, conditioners, and gels.

THE NIGHT TITI INTERRUPTED my sleep, she introduced me to what would become Curly Pudding, our first breakthrough hair-care product. But in the wee hours of the morning, neither Titi nor I could have known that this invention was to bring us equal amounts of joy and despair. Over the next few years, Curly Pudding, and an entire line of Miss Jessie's products, would afford us opportunities we never imagined—financial stability and independence and hard-fought recognition for being pioneers of the emerging segment of the hair-care business called the "natural hair movement." We didn't know then how huge this moment really was. But we had an idea we were on to something that would make our salon customers happy.

Ever since we started focusing on curly hair, we'd been struggling to find the right products to use in our Bed-Stuy salon. Nothing was quite right, and we found ourselves shopping the shelves of drugstores for products that we could combine and mix, using them in some unconventional ways. What we needed was a styling product that was gelatinous, without the tight hold of a gel. The needs of particularly tight-textured curly hair—the type most common among women of color— were specific, because for it to look and feel good, there had to be moisture, shine, and hold all in one product, with just the right amounts of each.

It was frustrating to go through countless jars and bottles of creams, curl activators, mousses, greases, hair sprays, gels, conditioners, and oils, spending all that money on solutions that just weren't cutting it. In between salon visits, I wanted our clients to have hair that looked and felt good, in order to maintain their curl and look. So I told Titi: "We need to create our own product. Let's try and come up with our own exclusive salon formula."

Identify a need for a product and find a way to create it.

That was how it usually happened. I would come up with an idea, my big sister would take it to the streets, and then the two of us would come together and make it a reality.

We started by hitting the beauty supply store, buying up varieties of curl activators, grease for texture, hair spray for hold, oil for shine, fragrance, color, and conditioner. We spent our off days and nights mixing various concoctions at the small kitchen table of the one-bedroom apartment Titi occupied on the third floor of our brownstone. Once our day's work was over,

Titi would go off and experiment all night, trying the combinations on her own hair, which was right in the middle in terms of curly type, as a result of our renowned Silkener. It had the thickness and tightness of curl, neither too unattainably slinky nor too kinky, making it the perfect "test case" for our average customer. Once she determined that the formulation was good enough, she would come down to the salon floor and we would test it on our consenting customers to get their feedback. Our clients weren't shy about telling us what was working and what wasn't. After that, I would test it on myself, getting up close and personal with our concoctions. It was the beginning of our research and development.

The problem with these products was that the hard gels were drying and made curls look too dry and crunchy. The alternative, grease, made them look wet and greasy. About three months after we started on this mission, Titi had a breakthrough and came up with a crème formula that was just right.

Once Titi mastered the texture, we spent more time together at the kitchen table fine-tuning, to get the color and fragrance right. This was almost as important as the function of the product, because it had to appeal to the senses.

As consumers ourselves, we know that women feel an emotional connection to their beauty products, and scent is such a critical component in boosting mood. Put simply, it had to smell yummy.

It also had to smell different from the usual brands marketed to women of color. Typically, these products had scents heavy on the bergamot or sulfur, or sweet fragrances such as coconut or cherry, which smelled more like cough syrup. It was a cliché, and we wanted to give our customers another option.

We sniffed a million scents before we finally chose more of a
fresh and fruity smell. Still delec-
table, with its food association,
but unusual. And unlike every-

Customers should associate your product with something delicious.

thing else on the market. It was strong and distinctive; women
either loved it or hated it. But many of our fans later reported
that it had an almost aphrodisiac effect on their husbands and
boyfriends, which couldn't be a bad thing!

The next and final element was the color. One of the things
we used to notice about Miss Jessie: When she was mixing a
cake batter or putting together a big Sunday meal, she was always big on presentation. Every detail, from how that cake was
frosted to the way those sweet potatoes were spooned onto a
platter, mattered. The food we ate not only had to taste good,
it had to look pretty. We took that lesson and applied it to our
formulation when we came up with a beautiful violet color.
Again, it was a completely different look from anything already
out there for curly hair.

Finally, with those pieces of the puzzle perfected, Titi had
cracked the code. We were both so excited, we couldn't get
back to sleep. We knew we had it.

★ ★ ★

Two

DEEP ROOTS

You don't choose your family.
They are God's gift to you, as you are to them.

—DESMOND TUTU

When I think back to our early childhood, growing up in Jamaica, Queens, in the seventies, long, shining, thick, straight hair is what I remember most. Our Japanese-American mother wore her jet-black crowning glory parted in the middle and cascading like velvet curtains halfway down her back. She used to wash it just about every day with Herbal Essences shampoo—the original emerald-green version in the bottle with the image of the woman in the Garden of Eden. Even now, when I come across that earthy, woodsy scent, it

evokes memories of my stunning young mother—a cool hip-
pie beauty—as she swung her wet hair from side to side to let
it air-dry.

Our mother was my childhood ideal. I know most children
remember their mothers as being beautiful, but those faded old
photographs confirm it. She was exquisite, with luminous yellow skin and almond-shaped eyes framed by perfectly arched
eyebrows. I remember her clicking around in high heels to
heighten her perfectly proportioned four-foot-eleven frame.
Her nails were sometimes painted red, her outfits occasionally
accented with a silk scarf or a floppy hat. My mother wore very
little makeup other than a swipe of lipstick and some blush if
she was going out. She didn't need to, because her striking and
delicate features, set in a heart-shaped face with high cheek-
bones and a rosebud mouth, were reminiscent of an Eastern
version of Vivien Leigh in her heyday.

Of course, back then I didn't draw that comparison. To Titi
and me, our mother looked exactly like the curvaceous Asian
woman who danced on *Soul Train*—Cheryl Song. It was as if
this foxy lady on the television were our mother's twin! The
two of us used to get excited when Kenneth Gamble and Leon
Huff's "TSOP (The Sound of Philadelphia)" theme song for
Soul Train came on. We'd run into the living room and dance to
the Jackson Five, Gladys Knight, and the Spinners, our father
teaching us all of his moves. But the best part was watching
Cheryl Song hustle down the *Soul Train* line in front of the
camera, swinging that hair back and forth. It made me feel
proud to think we had our very own version of the dancer right
there at home.

HARD TO HOLD

★

When my mother was at home, she was always this quiet, slightly aloof figure, more absent than present, always going off to work or school or her Buddhist group. We knew she loved us, but that warmth was missing, and we never quite felt like we could touch her. Instead, she was this elusive figure who floated in and out of our lives—an unattainable beauty in every sense.

That's why any attention we got from her felt extra good. It was girl time, and we could never get enough of it. Titi and I especially loved it when she braided our hair, decorating it with ornaments and colored beads. She used to buy Butterick patterns to sew matching outfits for our parties and school fashion shows, and they made us feel so pretty. She even made us jewelry by bending a fork into a funky bracelet, which we wore with pride. Our mother's attention was what we craved, especially her gentle touch when handling our unruly, thick-textured hair—the opposite of hers.

Typically, it was Daddy who took on the hair and wardrobe job in the mornings. It fell on him to get Titi and me ready for day care—this big man with big hands who just didn't have the skills. He used to pick out our kinks with a metal pick that had a wooden handle, and it hurt like hell when he pulled it through our hair, stinging our tender scalps. Titi, whose hair is thicker and denser than mine, was extremely tender-headed, and he used to hit her with the wooden part of the pick to stop her from crying and ducking. While he was busy with my sister, I used to try to beat him to it, rushing into the bathroom to wet and grease down my hair and pull it into two pigtails to avoid his torture—hence my early interest in hairstyling. But that wasn't the worst of it. Because our father didn't know what to do with all that hair, we turned up in day care with these huge Afros. At the time, it was embarrassing.

"You better stop that crying," he told us one morning as he was dropping us off for the day.

"But we look so stupid, Daddy," I told him, sniffling. "Everybody is going to tease us."

"That's all right—it's the style! Everybody who knows what's happening wears a 'fro," he said, trying to pass his handiwork off as style.

We knew better, even then. Titi let it roll off, but I desperately wanted to be that perfectly groomed little girl. I wanted to look like my early ideals of beauty and style: Donna Summer, Lola Falana, Cher, Diana Ross, Thelma from the TV show *Good Times*, and of course, my mother. At the time, I didn't fully understand my multi-textured curly and kinky hair from my mixed-race heritage as the blessing it was; I was too preoccupied with wanting to look like my mother.

AN UNUSUAL MIXTURE

★

That unconventional upbringing truly was a gift, allowing Titi and me to form opinions and an aesthetic sense that stood apart, even when we were children. Our worldview was shaped by two strong and distinct personalities: our parents'. Our father, Jimmy Branch, a six-one, handsome, and charismatic

black man, met our mother, Karen Matsumoto, in the late sixties in California at a taco stand. She was just sixteen going on
seventeen, the second-generation daughter of a protective and
traditional Japanese-American family. Shy, ethereal, and artistic, our mother captivated our father from the jump with her
beauty and intellect. At twenty-four, he had been something
of a ladies' man who usually went for much older and more
sophisticated women, but he fell hard for this strange and stunning young woman.

Even in the free-loving days of flower power, their mixed-
race romance broke all the rules. When our mother brought our
father to her parents' house for the first and last time, her uncle
kicked her right in front of him.

About a year after they met, while they were still in Los
Angeles, Daddy's young bride got pregnant with Titi. They
moved east to have the baby, and a year and a half later, when
our mother was just twenty, I was born. Even our names were
different from the norm. Our mother wanted to pick something
of African origin for her firstborn, so she chose the Nigerian
name Titi, after a beautiful African girl who was her friend in
college. It was typical of the. thoughtfulness our mother put
into everything she did. She loved the uniqueness of the sound
of that name, as well as its meaning, which, according to her
friend, was "wisdom," although other translations included "little flower." She picked Cree for Titi's middle name. As she explained to us later, "Choosing a Native American tribe's name
was to give a connection to this land."

For the same reason, my own middle name is Shawnee.
But since Titi had been given an African name, our mother
wanted to give me a name of Japanese origin. She chose Miko

for its sound and uniqueness. As she told me recently, "In Japanese, the same-sounding word can have a different meaning depending on the *kanji* character with which it is written. One meaning for Miko could be 'beautiful child' or 'female shaman.'" Apparently the name was typical of the women who served in Shinto shrines.

Incorporate your unique life story into your business dreams.

We were proud of our African-American/Japanese-American heritage. Needless to say, there weren't a lot of Titis or Mikos running around our neighborhood or schools. Nothing about my sister and me blended in, but we never felt the need to be followers. Our parents certainly weren't.

EARLY STRUGGLES

★

When I think about our parents in the first few years of their marriage, I can't help but think of that song "I Got You Babe," by Sonny and Cher: "They say our love won't pay the rent." Mommy and Daddy had love, and they had each other, but not much else. Financially it was tough, because Daddy left high school early to join the air force, served his time, and got out without two dimes to rub together. Then he fell in love and started a family before he had the means to support us. But he always knew how to survive. Although he eventually became an educated man, he had hustle and learned his survival skills from the street, watching the old cats play dice and listening carefully to what they had to say. He wasn't into anything illegal, but he kept his eyes and ears open for the next opportunity.

Not that he was consistent with his hustle. For all his fierce independence, Daddy did not always get money to pay for the kind of lifestyle he wanted for us. When we were babies, our father took us all to Poughkeepsie to Miss Jessie's house to get a home-cooked meal. In fact, I was born in Poughkeepsie, and the three of us—me, Titi, and our mother—lived with Miss Jessie for six months. Daddy stayed in the city during the week, because that was where he could find the opportunities, working as an insurance adjuster and driving cabs.

When we rejoined our father in New York, we continued to visit our grandmother a lot. He wanted to expose us to what he'd had, growing up in a home—a more wholesome and safe environment, a place where we could run around outside without worry. We'd been living on 137th Street in Harlem, when unemployment was high and muggings were commonplace.

It was a precarious start, but we didn't mind all the shuffling back and forth. Those early years around Miss Jessie's kitchen table were precious to us. "You gotta have common sense, remember that. Always use that God-given common sense," Miss Jessie made sure to tell us at every opportunity.

Our grandmother was old-school in the best possible way: a refined Southern belle who was an incredible homemaker. She didn't just fill us up with food; she made it her mission to fill us up with love and wisdom. It was the beginning of a huge role that our grandmother would come to play in our lives.

DADDY KNOWS BEST

★

Our father was the other dominant force. Daddy never babied us, even when we were babies. When we fell, he watched to make sure we got back up. When we were bad, he was tough, even resorting to the occasional ass-whooping to keep us in line. My sister and I had to make our own beds, put away our own toys, and take some responsibility for ourselves. Of course, he cared for us, making sure we were safe and had money for food (Mommy almost always did the cooking, cleaning, laundry, and food shopping). But Daddy treated us like little people, having real conversations with us about what to expect from life, and how we should conduct ourselves as young ladies. Most of all, he'd remind us to be independent. From the time we could crawl and put sentences together, he instilled that in us. It was like his mantra. "Miko, y'all got to understand that you should never depend on anybody. Always be independent," he told me. It sounded like a broken record to us at the time, but now, as a mother myself, I understand what our father was feeling. He was terrified. All around us were single moms struggling on their own, with babies to feed and husbands or boyfriends who'd left them. In the neighborhoods where we grew up, households where the men were around and providing for their families was not the norm. Daddy constantly worried that we'd become women who would depend on a man.

"You'll wind up alone, with no skills and no money, living in subsidized housing and buying groceries with food stamps.

"Nobody's an island, but at the end of the day, it's got to come through you," he told us. "Be self-sufficient; at least start from that point. You don't have to be a follower when you can do something for yourself."

"Need more; gotta have" was another one of his favorite sayings, echoing Miss Jessie, who always talked about the necessity of getting out there and earning the necessities and luxuries of life. She had no tolerance for entitled people who asked for things but weren't willing to work for them, and neither did our father. That's why, when Titi and I were six and five and we wanted to buy a plastic wading pool to cool off in, we ran a lemonade stand. That summer we raised twenty-five dollars—a fortune—to buy the pool, which was decorated with red and blue sailboats. Earning what you get was an important lesson for us. When Titi finally took the plunge in our backyard, it was a celebration. We'd never felt more pride of ownership.

Daddy was always striving to do better for himself and for us. It was a matter of pride and self-respect. That's why he was determined to buy a house for his family. Never afraid to take a risk, he waited until he and our mother got to the closing to tell the owners he had less than what they'd agreed to for the closing costs. Though it was a tactic to get the final number down, he truly did not have the money. The owners, desperate to close, agreed, and we moved to 127th Street between Linden Boulevard and 111th Avenue in South Ozone Park/ Jamaica in the early seventies. At first it was a predominantly white, lower-middle-class neighborhood, featuring rows of tract houses with neatly manicured front lawns bordered by wrought-iron fences. Before long, the demographics changed to mostly black and Hispanic. It was safe enough, and a much better place to raise a family than Harlem at the time.

Poor as they were, our parents were happy and carefree in those days, socializing with friends and throwing parties on weekends for no reason other than to dance and engage in interesting conversation. By then, our mother was studying at the School of Visual Arts in Manhattan while our father, who doted on her, financed her education as well as his own. It was an environment of creativity, spontaneity, and love. Mommy and Daddy were hippies of a sort, always wearing musk and patchouli oil and burning incense, although anyone who walked into our home could tell they had a kind of modern style.

Our Queens home was sparse, simple, and clean. My mother's vibrant abstract art hung on the walls, and the few items of furniture—two modern brown couches, a three-seater and a two-seater, and a large chrome reach-over lamp like the kind that's retro-cool now. The whole arrangement was tied together with a large piece of jewel-green satin fabric that covered the ceiling in a way that was typical of my mother's minimalist Japanese aesthetic. The kitchen was decorated in elaborate wallpaper. I still have those silver, red, and black geometric shapes etched in my mind. Brick-red wooden benches sat in the nook for our rectangular kitchen table, with a modern lighting fixture hanging above. Our parents' taste and resourcefulness made us look as if we had money. Our home was different, minimalist and cool. When everyone else's house was hooked up with mirrored walls and plastic-covered furniture, we had another idea of what was stylish and beautiful.

DANCE TIME

★

Even though there was no money to speak of, we never felt poor because our parents always found a way to make us think that we were rich and unique by enriching our lives with things like exposure to art, culture, and different ways of thinking. We always had music in our lives courtesy of our father. Those soulfully creative album covers of the Ohio Players, the Isley Brothers, and Barry White remain committed to our memories, evoking a time of innocence and joy. One image in particular, of a stunning bald woman with a perfect body and an expression of pure ecstasy, stands out. Another featured a Glamazon pouring honey all over herself. Looking back, I realize those images were racy, and that Titi and I had no idea what they were trying to evoke. We simply added these sexy women to our growing mental file of style icons.

Daddy always played music in the mornings, at night, and on weekends. Stevie Wonder; Donny Hathaway; Earth, Wind & Fire; and Marvin Gaye were some of his favorites. The full album would flow on our record player from front to back, and he made sure we could "catch the beat" when he held impromptu dance contests in our backyard.

OUR OWN

★

As much as we struggled, our father, a determined, proud, and hardworking man, was adamant that we get by on our own.

It was always about making do with what we had. I even re-member my father turning on all four stove burners and the oven to heat the house when we couldn't afford to turn up the thermostat.

Welfare was never an option. We were not allowed to get free breakfast and lunch at the public school on the corner, while all the other kids on the block could. We used to watch with envy as they drank the orange juice and ate the Frosted Flakes. Sometimes they even got pancakes. "Daddy, why can't we eat free food, too?" Titi ventured to ask. "Everybody else does."

"Don't set yourself up to have a welfare mentality," he snapped. "And don't worry about what everybody else is doing. I know one thing—you won't eat it. Getting something for noth-ing ain't shit."

DO THE RIGHT THING

★

Beyond the "no free meal" rule, our father never let us forget that you don't take what's not yours. We learned this lesson well when we were seven and eight years old and started hanging around Jeanette, a pretty Puerto Rican teenager who used to babysit us, give us baths, play games, and tell us stories about the boys she thought were cute. One day, for the first time, we decided to play hooky with Jeanette, ending up in a dime store on Liberty Avenue, where we stole makeup, hair accessories, and colorful plastic jewelry. It seemed like a fun day out until our father somehow discovered what we'd done.

"How was school today?" he asked us, playing dumb.

"It was good," we lied.

Before we could get the words out, the blows started coming at top speed. We got the ass-beating of our lives. His big hands alone were enough to inflict plenty of pain, but this time he took out belts, a wooden stick, and anything nearby to beat the shit out of us. Our father could hit hard, and his blows stung, and his words hurt even more. "I can't stand liars and thieves!" he screamed.

We cried as our mother stood off to the side, staying out of it. The next day he made an announcement: "Get all that shit together, because both of you are going down to Liberty Avenue to return every single thing you took."

He marched us into each store and made us tell the shop owner what we had done and how sorry we were. Jeanette faded to black from our lives; we were not allowed to even look at her from that day on.

JUST THE TWO OF US

★

As our distinctive little personalities were developing, we saw less and less of our mother. By the time we were six and seven, she was always either working or going to school. She started missing family holidays and staying away from us as she cultivated an all-consuming interest in Buddhism.

Her absence meant Daddy was the constant in our lives. He was our protector who took us to and from school. But he was also the oppressive alpha male who stuck to his role as authority figure, so we couldn't exactly talk or be too familiar with him. He had this unspoken rule that we could not get too mushy and affectionate by kissing or hugging him too much; we were also never allowed to sit on his lap. Years later we found out he never wanted any confusion about inappropriate behavior with his two daughters, since he knew he would be spending a lot of time with Titi and me. But this left us heavily codependent. For companionship and emotional support, we had only each other. "Two peas in a pod," our mother used to call us. And yet we could not have been more different.

Titi was the outgoing tomboy who was curious about the world and incredibly book-smart. Titi's kindergarten teacher, Mrs. Alexander, and first-grade teacher, Mrs. Selterman, constantly praised Titi for her incredible smarts and efforts at school. "I remember watching Titi do her homework in elementary school," Mommy shared with me years later. "I was amazed at how she had such clarity about her work assignments and, consequently, was able to organize and complete it with such swiftness."

I was always in awe of how quick Titi was able to make friends, easily engaging in conversations. Even as a child, she had a kind of innocent poise, asking questions and getting straight to the point without any inhibitions, in total contrast with my own shy and cautious demeanor. Always the center of attention, Titi had warmth and wit that made her incredibly popular among the other kids on 127th Street. Even though she was only a year older, she was very much the big sister, and I looked up to her. She often fought other kids for me, even the older boys who tried to bully me.

Maybe I was a target because I was seen as the docile girly girl who loved everything pink, held tea parties, and lived to make everything around me as pretty as could be. Happy in my own little bubble, I didn't try to fit in. I managed to make a few friends, becoming the go-to girl for hair if I was free to do whatever I wanted. One time a classmate allowed me to snip off her entire ponytail with a pair of paper scissors, leaving nothing but a short stub of hair sticking out from her elastic rubberband. I thought nothing of it until her mother came to the school the next day, furious about the little girl's new "do" and pointing at me across the room as the vice principal tried to calm her down. "Why did you cut my baby's hair like that?" she screamed at me.

I did not understand her fury and stood there, scared, with my mouth open. "I thought it was okay because she said I could cut it," I explained with tears in my eyes. The mother needed to be escorted out of the school because she was yelling so much and the two male gym teachers were sure she was going to hurt me bad. This particular lesson stayed with me for a lifetime: I always make sure to double-check how much is okay to cut before I start trimming.

I had more freedom with my sister's hair. Titi was always my willing guinea pig. As long as I had my sister, my dolls, my tea set, and a few items for hair and makeup to make everyone look pretty, I stayed out of trouble. Mostly, I was content to sit on the sidelines, looking out on the world from a safe distance—a state my mother called "inwardly attentive." Like Miss Jessie, I preferred the indoors. Daydreaming, playing with my mother's makeup, looking at magazines, and silently observing everything around me were more my speed.

It's all too easy to get pigeonholed when you are young. The truth about my sister and me was more complex; it always is. We weren't all one way or the other. Our whole lives, we took turns at being feisty and outgoing, introverted and gentle. We each had a little of Daddy, Mommy, and Miss Jessie's character, albeit with a dash more of some ingredients than others. And yet we always seemed to be the perfect complement, the ying to the other's yang, and an overwhelmingly positive force in each other's lives.

LATCHKEY KIDS

★

We also had each other's backs. If you messed with one of us, you messed with both of us. It had to be that way. We were latchkey kids who spent hours alone together, so the fact that we adored each other was a blessing.

Typically, we were left alone from three o'clock until dark, and to pass the time we would watch TV, even it was against our father's rules. As usual, he would find out, touching the TV when he came home to see if it was hot. He was strict with us because that was how he'd been raised by Miss Jessie. He never wanted us to feel like we could get too out of hand in his absence.

Not that he always played the heavy. He was the hands-on parent who did the occasional check-in on our homework, but he also made time to come up and make his presence be known at our schools. It wasn't unusual for our father to sit in the back of the class and observe. He was at every parent-teacher conference. He was also the parent who sits at the front desk in the halls—the first adult you see when you walk into a school. He always looked sharp, doing his volunteer school duty in a suit and tie.

Around the house, he always talked about how important his presence was, and, looking back, I see that he was right. By his actions, our father was demonstrating to everyone in our school and neighborhood that we had someone strong to look out for us. He made sure that no one—be they adults or other kids—would bother us. Never one to use soft or kind words, he showed his love through his protectiveness.

Not that his presence was consistent. When he had a deal to do, he'd be gone for hours. On weekends and evenings, when he had to handle his business, he'd leave us in his old tan Chevy, unattended for a couple of hours at a time. He never left the radio on, much less the air conditioner, though we at least knew to crack the window just enough to let air in. That alone time drew Titi and me even closer together. We talked about the future and the things we dreamed of accomplishing when we grew up. Both of us wanted to be businesswomen, although neither was sure what that entailed. We used to stare at the passersby and, based on how they were dressed and how their hair was done, try to imagine what they did for a living. Some of my fondest memories with my sister go back to those hours we spent watching people in the street from the backseat of our car, killing time, singing, playing pitty-pat, and laughing. A lot. We lived to entertain and please each other.

That backseat was almost like our very own after-school program, and Titi was my teacher and storyteller. She was intellectually curious, always reading and looking stuff up at the library. We had a set of encyclopedias at home, and she read just about every volume. On those long waits, she'd share whatever she'd learned in those books. I loved hearing Titi tell me all about Greek mythology: Pandora's box, Venus and Aphrodite.

THE SMART ONE

★

Titi's book smarts won high praise from Daddy. He always let it be known how proud he was of her. Her nickname was TCB, which stood not only for Titi Cree Branch but for "Taking Care of Business."

I also could not have been prouder of Titi. In fact, I was in awe of her. But her good standing with our father sometimes led to some hurtful comparisons. Because I was just an average student, he'd often say to me, "You can't get over by being pretty." That was his constant fear for us. He was deathly worried that I would rely on my looks and end up dependent on some man. He would highlight all the bad things that happened to girls who thought they were cute; sometimes his words bordered on cruelty. His constant criticism backfired in some ways, crushing my confidence by typecasting me as "the dumb one." It didn't exactly inspire me to do better in school.

Somewhat paradoxically, Daddy also drilled into our heads that we were "special, extraordinary, beautiful, and great." The word he loved to use was "exceptional." He talked about the importance of being free in our minds and always making decisions that would put us in a position of choice. He wanted us to develop minds of our own, and if he thought we were being followers in any way, he would make it difficult for us to be all right with that concept on the next go-round.

Education was extremely important to our father, who wore many hats, including schoolteacher. He eventually earned his master's degree in education, so academic excellence was high on his list of requirements for his daughters.

In the environment we grew up in, there were obstacles. Kids in Jamaica, Queens, could be rough at times, and there was no avoiding the occasional physical battle in school. One day in third grade, I came home to say, "Daddy, I got into another fight today."

"Miko, what happened? Who hit first?"

"She hit me first, and then I hit her back. The teacher had to break it up."

I needed to know how to fight in our neighborhood. I never went looking for trouble, but I stood my ground and learned to fight back when I had to.

This feisty streak surprised my father. He was trying to figure out if his daughter was a punching bag, a troublemaker or a stand-up girl. Not wanting us to have to fight our way through school, he quickly enrolled us in a program that bused us to an academically better elementary school in Whitestone, Queens—a predominantly white neighborhood with mostly Italian and Jewish kids. Titi was automatically put into the SP (advanced) class; somewhat surprisingly, I made it to SP class after a few months at school. Daddy was thrilled.

It was a big change from the school up the block. For starters, Whitestone was about an hour and a half away, and my sister and I had to walk thirty blocks, about a mile and a half, just to get to the bus stop. We loved the new school experience, especially Titi. She made friends with mostly Asian and white students who wanted to excel academically. We also had a group of friends from our 'hood, as we rode the school bus from Jamaica, Queens, to Whitestone. Even I did well at first, winning spelling bees and making A's, although I was always much more studious of human nature and soon immersed myself in the social aspect of school, getting to know the other girls from Whitestone and learning their ways.

Our new school provided a whole new cultural awakening. We heard unfamiliar terms and names like Guido, Guidette, and JAP (Jewish-American princess). I also made friends with girls who had names like Bethe Lacher, Margaret Randazzo, and Patty Comparetto. Whitestone was where I was introduced to Hello Kitty and Titi and I tasted our first Gummi Bears. I also got wise to the underhanded way girls tore each other down. In my experience in the mostly black neighborhoods like South Ozone Park, if girls didn't like you, they'd be direct about it. First there would be a verbal argument, then a minute to put Vaseline on faces for scratch protection, then an actual physical fight. Everything seemed to be pretty much over once the fight took place, with nothing left to guess about. But the mean girls at

Observe the people around you. It will help you better understand human nature and, in turn, your customer.

the white school would cut you dead in an altogether different fashion. It wasn't physical, and in many ways that was worse. Their beat-downs took the form of a silent treatment, followed by the spreading of a nasty rumor that would leave you completely iced out of the social circle. It was not unusual to be left alone at the lunch table if it was your turn to be "it." Isolation at its best.

I was especially fascinated by the different traits and characteristics of the various girl groups. If the subject of human nature had been on our school curriculum, no doubt I would have scored an A+. It gave me plenty of reference points later on in life, when I was doing hair, dealing with dozens of different women on a daily basis.

> *Be open to different experiences and receptive to the ideas of others.*

That knowledge would prove critical later on, when Miss Jessie's started interacting with thousands of women via the Internet, to introduce them to new possibilities with their hair. We quickly found out that in order to connect and reach these women, we needed to understand that it was less about hair and more about the psychology of different groups of women and their life experiences.

CHILD LABOR

★

School was only a small part of our education. When we weren't in class, our father put us to work in his new business, renovating and selling properties. Some of our earliest memories revolve around helping our dad.

"Titi, Miko, I need you to get in here and get this house straight so I can sell it," he'd tell us. Anxious to keep his overhead low, he kept the work in the family, having us spackle walls, paint, clean, and scrub floors, leaving us for hours to make these houses and apartments spotless while he went off to negotiate his next deal. It taught us a work ethic. We were eight and nine at the time, but it was another one of his life lessons. Our role as cheap labor went on for years.

Daddy was a good provider. Although he expected us to do our part, he carried most of the load. Our earliest memories are of him running between two or three jobs at a time. Daddy brought home anything and everything he could while out in the streets trying to make ends meet. At one point, he and an old man named Mr. James even rode down south to get a load of watermelons to sell out of Mr. James's truck on street corners in the neighborhood.

Daddy's drive to do better for himself, for all of us, was unrelenting. He was a young man coming up in the Civil Rights era, and he desperately wanted his daughters to have the kind of freedom and privileges that his generation had fought so hard for. That's why he was always drumming into us the importance of education, financial independence, work ethic, and grit.

Experience and education are the best teachers, even if the education is not formal.

On some level, his teachings must have sunk in. The hard-work habit has stuck, along with a fierce determination to be beholden to no one.

I learned from my foster mom, Grandma Sophie

MISS JESSIE'S HOUSE

around kitchen Table

Miss Jessie is one of the reasons we rarely gave our mother a hard time about being away so often on her Buddhist retreats. Our grandmother cooked, kept a clean house, and made it known on every level that family was her top priority. We learned everything we could from this gracious lady as we sat around her kitchen table. She was our foundation. All the down-home, do-right values that our father passed along to us originated from this wise and vibrant life force.

Born Jessie Mae Pittman in 1919 to a sharecropper family in Edgecombe County, North Carolina, she hated the outdoors. Proud, beautiful, and not a little bit vain, she didn't like the way the sun beat down on her creamy coffee-colored skin, much less breaking out in a sweat while working. She tried every trick she could think of to avoid picking cotton in the hot fields during harvest time. She quickly figured out that feigning illness was going to work only some of the time, so with a large family to feed—five sisters and one brother—Jessie Mae took over the kitchen. She was such an excellent cook, no one would dream of taking her out of the kitchen. She never had to pick cotton again.

She faced plenty of hardship growing up in the South during those years. Early on in Miss Jessie's childhood, her father, Rossi Pittman, remarried and relocated to Detroit. Her mother, Gertrude Pittman, married a man by the name of Alfred "Pap" Pierce, and the couple had four more children: Lillian (Sis), Ruth (Selma), Shirley, and Horace (Boy). Our grandmother used to tell us stories at her kitchen about how Pap gave preferential treatment to the three daughters he had with Gertrude, often at the expense of Miss Jessie and her whole sister, Bertha. And yet Sis, the eldest of the three half sisters, was crazy about Miss Jessie and would follow her around the house like a lost kitten. When they were older and Aunt Bertha had children of her own, Pap used to make her cook scraps on the little stove off to the side. She was forced to live on leftovers and never allowed to sit at the table and share a meal with the rest of the family.

Miss Jessie was allowed to partake in family meals only because she had become such a great cook, and it was her food Pap wanted to eat. Not liking how her sister was being treated, our grandmother made a point of saying at the top of her voice, "Now, Bert, you better stop all that crying! It don't make no sense to stick around here if you're going to be treated any ole kinda way. You need take your kids to get up out of here!"

GIRL WITH A GIFT

★

Miss Jessie herself was in no hurry to leave because she had a good job cooking for a well-to-do white family. The lady of the house taught her a thing or two about great food, and to some extent, Miss Jessie's skills were allowing her to, as she put it, "live the life of Riley." No one wanted to ruffle her feathers for fear she might boycott the kitchen. This was her gift, and it carried her through some tough times.

Our grandmother was such an artist when it came to cooking and making a home that, had she grown up in this century, she would have had her own catering company or restaurant. A visionary with a true entrepreneurial spirit, she figured out her talents and passions early on and honed her skills to perfection. It earned her an authority and respect at a young age.

Although she managed to complete a public school education, there weren't many options for a sharecropper's daughter coming up in the Depression, particularly a woman of color, so she did what most beautiful and talented girls did in those days: She got married. In 1936, at the age of seventeen, she wed Charlie Ann Branch—a military man—and had two children with him: Hilda and Jimmy, our father. When their marriage ended, our grandmother decided to take her kids to Poughkeepsie, New York, where a few of her cousins had already migrated. Charlie died soon thereafter.

Any skills you develop are yours to keep. They go with you everywhere, and no one can take them away.

But Miss Jessie was never alone for long. Defying the convention of the times, she moved in with George Dancey (Sweet), who fathered her two sons, Ricardo and Irvin. It was known that Sweet was a ladies' man, so that relationship didn't last, either. Miss Jessie set about raising her kids on her own.

Throughout, Miss Jessie was adamant about putting her children first. She did not care for how her mother, Gertrude, had allowed a new man to treat her and her sister, Bert. She stayed angry with our great-grandmother for years, and regarded her as weak for putting a man before her own kids. She made a promise to herself that if she had a family of her own, they would never have to wonder whether they were wanted or loved. She also made it clear that all of her children were whole brothers and sisters in spirit, whether they shared the same father or not. Miss Jessie despised anyone who put others before family. "Blood is thicker than water," she used to tell us, and she lived by that creed for the rest of her life.

Miss Jessie's nurturing skills were well known in the neighborhood. She was called the "cookinist" woman in Poughkeepsie. She stretched out a military widow's pension to feed and clothe everyone in her household. "How did she do it?" we once asked our father. "Sacrifice. Momma knew how to do without," he told us. "She always denied herself to make sure our bellies were full, our clothes were clean, and we had a warm, cozy house to come home to."

Miss Jessie's children were especially proud of the fact that their mother was such a famous beauty on the streets of Poughkeepsie. Aunt Hilda still remembers walking down Main Street one Mother's Day with Miss Jessie. "She literally stopped traffic, she had such a beautiful Coca Cola–shaped body," recalls Aunt Hilda.

NATURAL BEAUTY

★

Next to Mommy, our grandmother was my other ideal of feminine beauty. She had her own style that was as much about confidence and character as her considerable physical charms. Full-framed and shapely, Miss Jessie needed hardly any makeup, but a little eyebrow pencil and lipstick instantly turned her into a movie star with those big eyes, red-lacquered lips, and wide-brimmed black hats worn tilted to the side. She was a walking fashion mannequin, and her sartorial flourish was a quality our fly father has emulated to this day, with his collection of fedora hats, tailored suits, and painstakingly polished shoes. Daddy wanted to reflect some of Miss Jessie's star quality. No matter what was going on in her life, she always maintained her appearance, and so has he. It instilled in all of us a deep sense of pride and self-respect.

Miss Jessie also had a reputation for being incredibly tough. No one dared mess with her. She was very much in charge and a fierce protector of her children. One of the first stories Titi and I remember hearing about Miss Jessie involved our father when he was just a young boy. He came running up the stairs of their house on Bellevue Avenue, hollering, "Momma, that man who lives at the top of the hill just slapped me!"

"Oh Lord! Why did he go and do that?" Aunt Sis, my grandmother's sister, hollered from the other room.

Be your own best representative of your brand. Pay attention to how you dress and carry yourself. The manner in which you present yourself speaks volumes about your self-worth and can have a direct impact on your business relationships.

"I know damn well he didn't put his damn hands on my child!" Miss Jessie said. She couldn't get out of her housedress and into her street clothes fast enough. The man must have known Miss Jessie was coming his way, because he could hear her mouth from all the way down the street. But he was cool as a cucumber, as he leaned forward with his elbows resting on the banister of his second-floor porch, while Miss Jessie and Aunt Sis made their way up that long flight of stairs. As soon as she got up to him, she punched him all over his face and head, tearing him up while Aunt Sis held him down. She even twisted his cheek hard enough to draw blood. Aunt Sis was tall, big, and strong and could hang with the best of the men when it came to blows. She and our grandmother both knew how to fight.

Aunt Sis pitched in and started helping Miss Jessie with the beating. When our grandmother got tired of punching, slapping, and pushing the man, she told Aunt Sis, "Now throw his ass down the stairs!"

Once the man hit the bottom, they ran down and jumped on him again, kicking him everywhere and showing him no mercy as he yelled for help. When they were finished, they stepped over him and walked away, leaving the man in a fetal position on the ground.

"He better not never put his damn hands on not one of my kids—and I mean it!" Miss Jessie shouted, loud enough for the whole neighborhood to hear.

My father used to love telling that story. It was a reminder to all of us that you have to be fearless. My grandmother and her sister were two defenseless women raising children on their own, but their self-belief and desire to protect their own made them strong. The lesson stayed with Titi and me throughout our lives, especially as our business grew and we had something valuable to protect.

Do not mistreat others. Show them through your gracious actions how you expect to be treated.

BRINGING THE BACKBONE

★

Miss Jessie's no-nonsense approach to discipline was well known. She kept her children squeaky clean and well fed but was known to "tear ya behind up" if she had to. She insisted on two things for her children: good manners and good grooming. Miss Jessie was, above all, a lady. But she also instilled a sense of backbone and taught her babies to stand up for themselves, how "not to take no stuff."

The rules of behavior notwithstanding, we felt a freedom at her place and loved running outside in the fresh air. Miss Jessie loved us equally and kept a watchful eye on all of her grandchildren while we played outside in the Charles Street houses. One day she was watching out the window from her favorite easy chair—the one where she watched *The Price Is Right* and her "stories" —*As the World Turns, Another World,* and *The Young and the Restless.* Suddenly, she saw me rolling down a small hill fighting a boy named Stink. I was trying to defend our little cousin Chico—we cousins were close, and we protected one another no matter what. Seeing what was going down, Miss Jessie called Titi from the kitchen, where she was hot-combing her hair and said: "You better get out there right now and make sure Peanut [Stink's older sister] don't jump your sister, and I mean it!"

TO THE RESCUE

★

When Titi and I were thirteen and twelve, Miss Jessie came downstate to stay with us in Queens. I knew how much she hated to leave her home under any circumstances; we must have been in dire need of her help.

By then, our mother had moved to the premises of her Buddhist organization until our father moved out of the apartment. This lasted for a short while as our parents, who were separating, figured out the logistics of the family's living situation. As a result of all this back-and-forth, our dad found himself raising two girls alone, struggling to make ends meet. He needed our grandmother to cook, wash clothes, clean, and mind both of us. She lived with us for around three weeks, and we were in heaven! She showed us the love at breakfast, lunch, and dinner. She stocked the refrigerator with our favorite treats. Even better, she was a maternal fixture in the household: someone to come home to.

KITCHEN TABLE WISDOM

★

Except for that one blissful period when we had her all to ourselves, Miss Jessie was the larger-than-life woman who took us in over the holidays—Easter, Christmas, and Thanksgiving— any occasion that brought us together as an extended family. We felt enveloped in her love the minute we walked in the door. When we were little, it was our grandmother who made sure our hair was done right—washing, conditioning, braiding, or blow-drying it straight. She sent us to Kim, the daughter of her friend Miss Carrie Mae, to get our hair corn-braided; later, she would send us to Miss Vivienne to get cholesterol deep treatments and roller sets.

We spent as much time at her house in Poughkeepsie as we possibly could, relishing the scent of freshly folded laundry and a kitchen filled with the smells of all her specialties. There was always something good cooling on top of the stove or table—fresh-baked sweet potato pies, peach cobbler with a buttery crust in a large rectangle roasting pan, or our favorite, banana pudding. That was the way she expressed her abiding love to all of us. If she was an artist (and she truly was), the kitchen was her studio and the place where she found the source of her creative expression. It surely was her favorite room, and it was at her kitchen table that the two of us—Miss Jessie's "grandbabies from down New York"—learned some of our greatest values.

The biggest thing Miss Jessie taught us was how to identify a need or problem and then find a solution. "Just look around you," she'd tell us. "All you need is right there at your fingertips. If you just use common sense, you will get it."

That was Miss Jessie's approach to her recipes. She made mostly everything from scratch, never needing a recipe book. She used common sense to achieve her vision, whether it was the smoothest yellow cake batter, or an egg and mayonnaise treatment she whipped up to deal with our unruly hair. She had all these down-home Southern recipes and remedies for everything under the sun, whether it was a little lard or cooking oil to smooth down her own curls, a hint of nutmeg, cinnamon, and vanilla in her sweet potato pies, or a splash of lemon and vinegar to disinfect a floor.

Miss Jessie was the most resourceful woman we'd ever met, and she passed along many of her secrets. If she couldn't find it on the store shelves, she'd add a little of this and a little of that to create something that met her exacting standards. Whatever worked, Miss Jessie would find a way.

STRETCHING A DOLLAR

★

There was very little money coming into Miss Jessie's house, although you'd never know it based on the sense of abundance her environment evoked. Whenever she needed more cash, she sold a few of her delicious pies out of her home, one of the many ways she found to make ends meet. She was a proud woman who never complained. Miss Jessie had no time for victims. That self-respect was reflected in her surroundings, which were immaculate. The place was always scrubbed clean, with sharp elegant furnishings our aunt Hilda picked out for her.

Miss Jessie bragged to all of her friends about how fabulous her wall-to-wall black velvet couch was, accented with oversize dark teal lamps and hints of blue in the drapes and pillows. Our grandmother didn't need wealth to live richly. She could stretch a dollar to cook a feast for twelve people. She could make a bed with crisp sheets and perfect creases on the corner of a mattress. She could present herself like the refined lady she was, styling her limited staple of outfits with a pretty blouse, beautiful hats, flawless makeup, and not a hair out of place—and all of this was accomplished with one arm.

People did not think of her as disabled in any way, because she compensated by doing more than most would with two arms. She could peel all of her potatoes. Chop every last one of her onions and vegetables. Even knead the dough for her pies. And as all of her kids knew, she could beat your ass with that one arm, too.

We were too busy passing her a pan, a bag of flour, or anything Miss Jessie asked for in her kitchen to ask her how she managed. Instead, she showed us. Miss Jessie could delegate as well as any top CEO. You could not be a bump on a log around our grandmother. But we would do anything for the chance to be in that space, absorbing all of her wisdom.

> *Don't adopt a victim mentality by blaming others or feeling sorry for yourself. Embrace and plan for victory.*

One of the few things she struggled with was getting her hair just right. She could comb it through, but not the way she liked. Whenever she needed a roller set, she'd have to call one of the grandkids or daughters-in-law to roll up her hair. She was sure to protect her hairdo in a satin cap at bedtime. She avoided the rain and did everything she could to make her curls last until someone came to roll again in the next week or two. It's partly why, when we got older and I was doing hair myself, Miss Jessie was excited by our weekend visits; she couldn't wait to get her hair done. In fact, she counted the days, calling Daddy to say, "When are y'all coming? I need to see my girls—I want to get my hair done!"

Even in elementary school, I was experimenting with hair and, with the exception of that one incident with the paper scissors, getting good at it. Our bedroom at home was starting to look like the back room of a salon, full of my grandmother's old wigs on Styrofoam heads, brushes, hot combs, beads, and hair accessories. I was always wetting down my own hair with water, Dixie Peach pomade with lanolin, Blue Magic hair grease, or Dippity-do gel, to see what looks I could come up with. When I wasn't practicing on myself, Titi was my go-to model for different looks. Eventually, I would give all of my friends and relatives their first relaxers and haircuts. I'd gained something of a reputation as the Branch family hairstylist, and my services were always in demand.

After we ate a good meal was Miss Jessie's time to get her hair done. It was always a team effort: I relaxed and trimmed our grandmother's hair. Titi assisted, washing out Miss Jessie's long silver hair and coating it with a concoction of eggs, mayonnaise, and vegetable oils that she prepared and mixed according to our grandmother's precise instructions.

We cherished those times with our grandmother. She was giving us the girl time and attention we'd craved from our mother. Miss Jessie wasn't much for hugs or saying "I love you," but she didn't have to. We knew it. We had our own love affair with our grandmother, apart from our parents and the rest of the family, when we would sit at the kitchen table, listening to her stories, laughing, and soaking up everything she said and did.

As much as Daddy drummed into us the importance of

being self-sufficient and free in our minds, it was Miss Jessie's constant positive reinforcement of family and outward display of love that resonated with us at the time. Above all, she gave us a blueprint for the women we wanted to become: family-centered, proud, hardworking, independent, and never failing to create something extraordinary—from scratch.

★ ★ ★

Three

STREET WISE

You must learn.

—KRS ONE, BOOGIE DOWN PRODUCTIONS

O ur father was not playing. "Miko! Where's Titi at?" he demanded, the veins popping up on his left temple.

I was in my bedroom, experimenting with cutting the top of my hair in short layers while I left the back long, and it took some concentration, so I was annoyed by the interruption. "I don't know!" I said, rolling my eyes when I was sure he wasn't looking.

"You better not know, because if you do, I'mma put my foot in your ass!"

I knew then that I was about to get the full brunt of his wrath for something Titi had done.

"Again, I'm going to give you one more chance to tell me where she is," he said, pointing his big finger in my face.

I had a rough idea where my sister might be, but I was not about to assist in getting my sister's ass beat, because I knew what could happen if he found out. The thought of witnessing the screams and blows raining down on my big sister made my stomach hurt.

Titi was in love with a guy in St. Albans, clear on the other side of Queens. His name was Justice, although his government name was Robert. Justice was the name he'd gotten as a member of the Five-Percent Nation, an Afrocentric offshoot of the Nation of Islam founded in Harlem in the sixties. In his downtime, he was referred to as GOD, which was what all the Five-Percenters called themselves.

It was one of many community movements picking up among young black and Hispanic men and a few women when we were coming up in the eighties, and a lot of our friends from school and around the neighborhoods were down with it. References to it by hip-hop MCs at all the block parties, and later affiliations with early rappers like Big Daddy Kane, Rakim, and Wu-Tang Clan, gave a nod to Five-Percenters.

Kids were finding their identities in all kinds of ways—rapping, break-dancing, tagging, being Five-Percenters, or all of the above. Titi had found the whole package in Justice, and our father didn't like it one bit.

Somehow, Daddy guessed where Titi was. She just wanted to hang out for a few hours with the boyfriend she'd been banned from seeing, so she sneaked out that evening and took the bus to his house. Determined to find her, Daddy got in his car, drove around the neighborhood half the night, and after asking a few folks on the corner, managed to hunt down where Justice was living. Daddy banged on the door. Justice's parents let him in, and Dad came crashing down the stairs to the basement, where Titi was hiding under the bed.

"No, Dad, noooo! I wasn't even doing anything!" Titi protested.

"Didn't I tell you not to run around with this dude? Didn't I tell you to stay your ass home?" Daddy yelled. "Git your ass up!" he demanded. Then he dragged her out of her hidey-hole, up the stairs, and out of the house. Once he had her in his clutches, he grabbed her up in front of the whole street.

It was his way of helping Justice understand that Titi had a father who did not play. The message was received. Our boyfriends sure were scared of our father, although not as frightened as Daddy was at the thought that his thirteen-year-old baby girl was stepping out with a seventeen-year-old young man at the dawn of the crack era.

A NEW ERA

★

Our teen years were an era of discovery for us, a time when kids all over New York City were finding forms of self-expression. Growing up in Queens in the eighties was a blessing, because we got to be there at the birth of hip-hop, a time of experimentation in art, music, fashion, and entrepreneurship like we'd never seen. The music movement was starting just as we were hitting puberty in 1979, with disco and songs like Chic's "Good Times" phasing out, and rap just getting on the radar with Bronx DJs and groups like the Sugar Hill Gang. It was all connected. The Sugar Hill Gang's "Rapper's Delight" even sampled Chic's "Good Times" —the bass line that carried what is arguably the original rap song.

The first time we heard that record, we were on the school bus from Jamaica to Whitestone, and it was so popular that everyone knew the rhymes by heart. On those long rides into Whitestone, we would also listen and jam to Grandmaster Flash and the Furious Five on a huge beat-box radio that one of the other kids brought on the bus. By then, some of the girls had started wearing Jheri curls and would be sure to get teased if they leaned their head on the bus window and left a big grease stain.

By the time we were in junior high school, hip-hop went local, and a lot of talent came out of Queens. Hollis, in particular, was a hotbed of talent, with Jam Master Jay, Darryl "DMC" McDaniels and Joey "Reverend Run" Simmons from Run DMC and of course, LL Cool J. Other parts of Queens turned out talent like Roxanne Shanté, and Marley Marl, and Sweet Tee. When we were in high school, there were Salt 'N Pepa, Biz Markie and Nas from Queensbridge and, from St. Albans, Q-Tip and Phife Dawg of A Tribe Called Quest. One after the other, new rap groups were coming on the scene, and just by living in Queens we had access to them all. It wasn't unusual to see these MCs and rappers out in the streets.

It was something we took for granted, growing up in the city, with music and culture on our doorstep. It wasn't just the music coming out of Queens and taking over. Entrepreneurship was in the air, with Russell Simmons from Hollis cofounding Def Jam Recordings and turning an underground movement into mainstream business. Being born into this helped us to see what could be done. The fear of trying was never there.

Many businesses were being born from that time and place. Through music and fashion, there was a pride and spirit associated with black entre-preneurship just emerging from the streets of Queens, Brooklyn, Harlem, and the Bronx. We were growing up with these young men. Daymond John, founder of FUBU, or For Us By Us—one of the first multimillion-dollar hip-hop clothing lines—went to high school with us, as did his business partners. Apparently, by breathing the same air and drinking the same water, we were influenced by incredible talent and raw entrepreneurism, blessed as we were to be living in one of the most creative cities in the world.

> *Sample and curate experiences, trends, and ideas. They will inform you as a tastemaker.*

OUR OWN LANE

★

By then we were living in a middle-class section of Flushing. Our family had moved from Ozone Park, a section of Jamaica, Queens, in 1980, when we were ten and eleven. Our mother insisted we be around a broader mix of ethnicities. Jamaica was predominantly black and Hispanic, while Flushing had every hue and ethnicity, including more Asians.

In retrospect, it was a good move for us, because a lot of

kids coming up in a more ethnically homogenous neighborhood got locked into one way of thinking. Some of them never left their four corners in Jamaica. Flushing was a whole different vibe. Because we were being bused to a white school in Whitestone with kids from other neighborhoods, we were still making friends and staying connected with people from Jamaica, St. Albans, Laurelton, and Hollis. We maintained roots while constantly forming new social networks. It wasn't just one tight circle but many. We never stayed in one spot; we ping-ponged among all the neighborhoods where we knew people.

We were developing our own identities, each of us in our own lane. Titi and I were close, but we never felt the need to cling to each other. It wasn't the same codependency we had when we were little girls. Now we were old enough to take public transportation and travel around unsupervised. (In the eighties, kids were much less coddled, and twelve- and thirteen-year-olds were considered old enough to take a bus on their own.) Being more mobile opened up our worlds. We had a few friends in common, but mostly, we did our own thing, coming together to protect and support each other on an as-needed basis.

TEENAGE REBELLION

★

As usual, Titi was the adventurous and bold one, always throwing herself headlong into whatever new thing was happening in the neighborhood. She preferred to trust people—or at least give them the benefit of the doubt—experiencing something first and then reflecting on it later. In that sense, she was the exact opposite of me. I tended to play everything out in my head beforehand, analyzing each and every move like a chess player.

Titi's free-spirited ways were causing some concern for our father, because she was getting so deep into the school of life that her regular studies had fallen by the wayside. Titi cut so many classes that she got kicked out of Hunter College High School, the special school where she'd been placed for being exceptionally bright. Her teachers never got to know of her keen intellect. In her own way, she was rebelling against Daddy's strict rules. Besides, there were too many other interesting things going on in the streets around her. At that age, Titi couldn't have cared less about her academics. Her interest in people had kicked in.

I watched, taking it all in and calculating my risks. Only once, when I was fourteen, did I get in over my head. I'd been hanging out at my girlfriend's house, where her cousin and my boyfriend, Sayquann, met us, and I didn't get home until three A.M. My father didn't approve. He smacked me hard the moment I came through the door, knocking the earring right out of my ear. I was never allowed to go back to that house again.

For the most part, I stayed out of trouble. After I'd seen Titi catch hell with our father, mine was a much more quiet rebellion. I was hell-bent on avoiding Titi's more overt mistakes, while asserting my individuality in other, more subtle ways. Titi's rebellion was in her actions, mine was in my head, and in a way that was more dangerous. There was no longer anything docile about this girly girl, who obviously had inherited Miss Jessie's feistiness.

CLOSE CIRCLE

★

I thought my sister was "out there" for someone our age, so I usually tried to stay inside the lines with a small tight-knit circle of friends who were a little less wild and more age-appropriate.

Neal Jackson, my classmate and constant companion throughout junior high and high school, shared my love of music and fascination with human behavior. Creative and witty, with a flair for writing and other forms of self-expression, he had a sense of style all his own. Neal was the person I checked in with every day. Next to Titi, he was the friend who knew me best. Years later, he would become our future promotions consultant at Miss Jessie's.

Everyone in our orbit had a creative side. Either we were drawn to them, or they were drawn to us. My friend Tony Bodden used to rhyme and even had his own group, with hip-hop producer Irv Gotti as his MC and beatboxer Rahzel, who eventually joined the Roots. They were so good that whenever they played, word of mouth would spread and they'd fill the stadium at Jamaica Park. Tony's crew won rapping contests and even got a recording deal. Rumor had it that Run DMC wanted to record with them. Later on, Tony cowrote the screenplay for Hype William's movie, *Belly*, starring Nas, DMX, T-Boz, and Method Man.

Neal was heavily into the music, eventually leaving the neighborhood to tour with his sister, Toi Jackson, aka Sweet Tee, one of the first female rappers to get a recording deal, with her hit "It's My Beat." Neal, who shared stories from his touring days, learned a lot from the music industry that he would later apply to Miss Jessie's marketing campaigns.

BIG BRO'

★

The one dear friend Titi and I had in common was Joseph Handy, another St. Albans boy who became a kind of big brother to us. Titi, Joe, and a few others became especially close, doing everything together, including cutting class, smoking weed, riding the 7 train into Manhattan, dancing at block parties, and sneaking off to see the Diana Ross concert in Central Park.

Joe embodied so much of what was going on in that era, rapping with Justice, Titi's former boyfriend; wearing his shell top, Adidas, sweatsuits, and Kangol hats; and tagging graffiti all over the place with his crew of friends. We were excited for him when we saw him rhyming at the Apollo Theater in Harlem. Today he is a graphic artist and sometimes does illustrations for Miss Jessie's—one of a handful of creative friends from back in the day who now have a connection to our business.

FASHION, HAIR, AND HIP-HOP

★

Our own self-expression took the form of fashion and, of course, hair. We rocked that whole eighties look, shopping at

VIM and the Colosseum Mall on Jamaica Avenue. Titi had a gray sheepskin, and I had a black "goose" bomber jacket from Delancey Street.

Trying out the different hair and style trends was one way we had fun together. I'd do Titi's hair, and we'd borrow each other's clothes and jewelry. Sometimes it led to fights if one of us lost something or took some earrings without asking. Make no mistake, we were adolescent girls who had our share of fights about stupid stuff. But experimenting with the different looks of the eighties and early nineties was how we bonded as sisters. We cultivated our individual looks, but we were each other's best critics, and neither of us would let the other out of the house looking anything less than fly and stylish. On rare occasions we even dressed in the same clothes, or complementary color combinations, like identical twins. It was something we did playfully, just to mess with people. We were the Branch sisters out in full force.

My sister and I preferred to set the trend rather than be a part of one. We liked to mix various elements to make them our own. Many of the girls rocked sweatshirts with felt letters on the front and back, stating their crew, zodiac sign, or even their 'hood. They would pair them with Lee jeans, a name belt and Adidas shell-top sneakers or Reebok high tops, also known as Fifty Four-Elevens (because with tax they cost exactly $54.11). We loved that style a lot, but when others went right, we went slightly to the left. We took a peek at what was happening in the street culture, filed the information we needed,

When it comes to trends, you don't have to be all in. Take what works for you and discard the rest.

and traveled on. It's how we've operated throughout our career, never going too deep into lifestyle. This approach has allowed us to stay outside trends and provided us with a view of what was on the horizon.

Not that we didn't have fun with whatever was happening in the moment. I was doing the sexy punk Madonna thing—lots of bracelets, lace, fingerless gloves, neon socks, and thrift store finds, which was odd for a black girl in those days. Titi and I moved on to the next look quickly. At an early age, we were influenced by many groups that seemed to be worlds apart, even the middle-class kids in Whitestone who were rocking Benetton shirts buttoned all the way up to the collar, and Adidas Stan Smith tennis shoes.

We became vessels for all these different looks. We would express ourselves by blending everything to come up with our own style. Our black, white, Asian, and Latino friends could never completely understand what we were doing, as it was impossible to put us into any single category.

In the eighties, the look for black girls' hair was starting to get more interesting. It opened the door for experimentation. These were the days before we could afford to go to the salon for relaxers, so we hot-combed it straight instead. Our mother was the first person to ever straighten our hair, using a lot of Dixie Peach pomade. We became pros at doing our own hair, heating our combs on the stove to iron it bone-straight while greasing it with oil. Not lard; not petroleum jelly. Oil. It was a little trick Miss Jessie taught us, because safflower or vegetable oils were much better for the hair follicles and less heavy. Our mother, being into natural ingredients, also had a stash of oils and essences that we used to raid. The oils worked, but the result could be some funky-smelling hair, like it'd been cooked in the deep fryer.

One time I left my brush at my then-boyfriend's. He picked it up, sniffed it, and said, "What the hell is that smell?" Later on, he grew to love that burnt-hair scent, but it wasn't exactly the perfumed hair we read about in romance novels.

In the early eighties, a standard look was the ponytail. We would wear it greased back or damped down with water to smooth out the texture. We wore our hair loose in the back with two cornrows against a side or middle part. We also wore beads and did our hair up in a turban-like style, tucking our hair around a tube top. The final effect looked something like a giant hair mushroom.

One thing nobody was doing back then was wearing it out and natural. Many girls were doing the Jheri curl that Michael Jackson was rocking, but some days I just let my hair go wet, wavy, and curly, a style now known as wash-n-go. It wasn't a total curly look—I groomed and conditioned my hair with mousse and conditioner—but it was a textured look that caught some attention. "Miko, do your hair in that frizzy look. I like that," my best friend, Neal, used to tell me. "It looks so different when you do that."

The age of innocence came to an end by the time we hit fifteen and sixteen, when so many of our friends got caught up in the drug game. The same boys we watched play handball in the park days turned up on the corner with BMWs and clothes just a little too fly for a sixteen-year-old from Queens with no job. By this time most of the guys had beepers on their hips. Many of our friends started experimenting with more than a little weed and graduated to the harder stuff by putting cocaine in their cigarettes, spliffs, and blunts. Some ended up getting hooked, and things got violent real quick.

BRANCHING OUT

★

When things took a turn, Daddy cranked up his protection mode, and we started focusing more on school. We grew to understand why he was being hard on us. There was a lot to save us from, but we'd already had enough of a foundation to know we were destined for bigger things. We also had each other.

This was during the Ronald Reagan era, when money was pouring into the city, and our mother and father were both starting to benefit. Our mother landed a job at Grey Advertising as an art director, and our dad, who by then was running Branch Realty out of a building in Rockaway that he'd bought a few years earlier, was having a good streak selling properties. He even sold the famed Lenox Lounge on Lenox Avenue in Harlem.

The prosperity was sudden. We went from making do to being picked up from Poughkeepsie at the end of one summer in Daddy's black four-door Mercedes-Benz. It was sharp and made him look even more like a million dollars. We took our first family vacations to St. Croix in the U.S. Virgin Islands, and Redondo Beach in California. Our apartment in Queens even got a face-lift. Our mother chose a well-designed and expensive black modular couch, brushed silver plush carpet, and exotic tall plants placed along windows accented with Levelor blinds. We bought new dishes and silverware, and our father treated himself to an expensive stereo system with a Technics turntable, an Akai receiver, and powerfully clear speakers that played his music morning, noon, and night. He especially loved Frankie Beverly and Maze, Alexander O'Neal, and retro albums like Marvin Gaye's *What's Going On?*

Titi was reaching college age and wasn't decisive about which school to attend. I urged her to consider the University of Maryland. It wasn't for the usual reasons, like academic excellence. The school caught my attention when I saw all of the excitement about Len Bias, who played on their college basketball team and was considered by many to be one of the greatest amateur players in the history of the sport. Everyone was buzzing about the University of Maryland because he had just been drafted to the Boston Celtics. I thought my sister could get a college education and not miss home too much because, for that reason alone, it seemed like a cool school.

We both got out of Queens and went to college. At Maryland, Titi studied consumer economics. I attended junior college upstate, at Hudson Valley Community College in Troy, New York, where I studied liberal arts. By that time it was safe to say we were looking for a fresher, more wholesome perspective on life—too many people in our world were dying.

Being away from Queens gave us a healthy dose of self-awareness and self-esteem. Always pegged as "the dumb one" by our father, I began acing my courses. Being away from Daddy's constant criticism inspired me to do well for myself, and

I flourished in that environment. Titi the rebel also knuckled down, rediscovering her giant intellect and diving into the kind of formal education that could bring her closer to her dream of becoming a businesswoman.

Then things took a turn. While Titi was away and I was in my last year of high school, the real estate market had crashed and, symbolically, our dad's Mercedes got totaled. It wasn't long before Daddy started reasserting his influence and direction. When we came back to Queens for the summer, he decided it was time for us to be put back to work. Not only did we have to get our real estate licenses to help him sell properties; the three of us needed to go into the cleaning business together.

Well, not together, exactly. For Daddy, our going into the family business meant free labor for him. He filed the incorporation papers on Branch Cleaning Agency while we rolled up our sleeves and went to work. It was his way of making sure we didn't have to work for other people. For our father, it was all about controlling his own destiny. Independence meant everything to Daddy, even if he had to sacrifice income and start all over again. It was how he was raised by Miss Jessie, who took fierce pride in being accountable to herself and never having to answer to a boss. This way, she never had to compromise her values.

Titi and I didn't question it. We thought, *How hard could this be?* We were no strangers to cleaning and always put our backs into it. We couldn't imagine the cleaning supplies costing too much, either. We were up for the job if it meant that we would be part of a successful business with our father.

ELBOW GREASE

★

The agency occupied a small room in his real estate business, which was located in a building that he owned on Rockaway Boulevard in Queens. Titi and I scored Branch Cleaning Agency's first job after canvassing Main Street in Flushing. The job was to deep-clean a dirty and unlivable two-story beach house in the Rockaways, top to bottom, for just forty dollars per floor. We scrubbed disgusting thick mildew in between tiles, cleaned mold and unfamiliar growths out of a refrigerator, scoured a rust-brown ring and film from a toilet bowl, purged out the urine smell that had seeped into the grout on the dirty tile floor. It was nasty, but the two of us worked our butts off and had that place sparkling clean. After we calculated time, gas, cleaning supplies, and labor, we realized we weren't left with much.

In the fall, Titi couldn't wait to go back to college, because Branch Cleaning Agency was hard work, although she did feel somewhat guilty about leaving me to carrying the load. "You gonna be all right?" she asked me.

I told her I'd be fine. I didn't feel I had much of a choice. If I gave up so easily, my father would see me as a failure, and I could not bear the idea of him placing me into a category of people who liked to work for others (even though I was effectively working for him). This wasn't just about living up to my father's expectations. Making the enterprise a success was about my own pride and dreams for my future as a successful and independent businesswoman.

By then my entrepreneurial fire was burning bright, and I

was determined to make it work. Eager to present myself in a more professional way and no longer choosing to work on the cheap, I designed a brochure for Branch Cleaning Agency and created the service menu for our business. I learned how to lay out this art by working part-time with my mother's graphic designer friends—a job I took to supplement my nonexistent income from our family business. I went door-to-door, handing out fliers in higher-income neighborhoods around Queens and Manhattan, and negotiated prices. It was all on me, because Daddy did not take this business seriously at the time; he was more preoccupied with reviving his real estate business.

Learning lessons from prior mistakes, I brought in cleaning jobs that ranged in price from three to four hundred dollars. At this point, it was all about knowing the value of my work. I had no intention of laboring for hours alone in some four-room house or office building for peanuts. My initiative drew the attention of my father. He saw that there was money to be made. Ever domineering, he stepped in and started telling me how business was supposed to be run. "Do this and do that! Don't do this and don't do that!" he would tell me. In this case Daddy was a great armchair CEO, but it wasn't going to fly this time, because I was the one who had to do all of the work. "Dad, I got this. Just let me do things this way—it works," I pleaded.

But he wouldn't listen. He kept coming in, trying to run things, and he was doing a masterful job of taking over, even though it was hardly helping the business.

I was frustrated. My success in college had given me a renewed sense of confidence, bolstered by all that I'd already accomplished in the Branch Cleaning Agency. I knew how to make money, and I did not agree with Daddy's direction, so we bumped heads all the time. I stood up for myself against the most intimidating alpha male I'd ever known, my father.

Contrary to the image I had of my father as a business-man, I was beginning to realize that he was not, in fact, the kind of businessman I wanted to emulate. He made money only to lose it again. He invested unwisely and missed all kinds of opportunities. He overspent and took too many risks. All too

Challenging life experiences make you a better business leader.

often his free-spirited approach to making a dollar lacked the neces-sary planning and organizational skills, which ultimately got in the way of his business sense. He had so much debt that our business had nothing to show for all the hard work. It was frustrating, and I felt defeated.

I saw the path I needed to take, and it went in the opposite direction from my father's footsteps. This was the first time I had a sense of who I was as a businesswoman. I knew what was true and what was not. Suddenly, I had an opinion about the manner in which I would operate a business on my own.

BUTTING HEADS

★

Not that Daddy was about to fold any time soon. He could be stubborn. Even though I was the one who had created the cleaning-business model from soup to nuts, Daddy would fre-quently take over my accounts, presuming he was in charge of the business I'd been building. He would negotiate lower prices with clients, undermining my pricing system. Too often he would spend money on supplies at a job site that would cut our cleaning income by half. Even though he thought he was doing the right thing, his actions infuriated me. I was doing all the manual work and getting the jobs, and he was blowing it.

This father/daughter tension dragged on for months. I could no longer abide Daddy's "pretty and dumb" insults. I knew I had earned my position as a valuable player. Determined to prove my father wrong, I went out and got more accounts at even higher prices. I'd caught the entrepreneurial bug and was making the point that my time and service were worth something. As a result, the business was succeeding, but every dime went into the debt that our father owed: parking tickets, mortgage payments, rent, utilities, and so on. We saw no light in this situation.

I became a prisoner of the business. Just twenty years old, I endured for no financial reward while missing out on my youth. I was completely cut off from all the fun our friends were having, partying and socializing. Culturally, times were changing; we were coming out of a Teddy Riley New Jack Swing era into a more grassroots, bohemian, open-minded and Afrocentric approach to rap and music. People traded in their gold chains and started wearing wooden beads. The Native Tongues—which included the Jungle Brothers, De La Soul, A Tribe Called Quest, Queen Latifah, and Monie Love, had become the sound of our generation. The music and culture were becoming more socially conscious and intellectual, and I was eager to be a part of them.

Understand the sacrifices as well as the rewards of becoming an entrepreneur.

The summer following the founding of our family business, Titi came home from school for good. What my sister saw shocked her, and looking at old pictures from that moment in time, I can understand why. I looked sad and worn out, with barely a flicker of spirit behind my eyes. Within a year, I'd gone from a trendsetting fashion plate to someone who lived in a cleaning uniform and sneakers. I even gained weight, turning to food to deal with the stress. Titi barely recognized her once cute and feisty baby sister.

"Miko, what happened to you? Why do you look like that?" she asked me when she walked in the door.

Seeing my older sister, ally and protector again, I felt a wave of relief. When you're building up a business, you can get so deep into it that you start believing it's all there is. But Titi reminded me there was a whole other world out there and that I was no longer alone in this.

REUNITED

★

We were a team again—a sister act. We fought with our father every day until we'd finally had enough. We left the business, which he eventually dissolved. By then, our parents had divorced and our father had moved out of the apartment. It was just me and my big sister, and it felt good to take charge of our lives. We were young women with our own ideas, more than capable of looking after ourselves.

We valued what he'd taught us, including how *not* to be in business. Working with our father showed us that it was possible to build something of our own. He gave us the opportunity to run a business. It wasn't in our name, nor was it something I would have chosen for a long-term career, but it sowed the seeds of self-esteem and ambition in me. It put us on a path.

I got clear on something else: I needed to have an all-consuming passion for the business I hoped to build. Being an entrepreneur requires long, hard hours, and I would need to wake up every morning excited to do all that was necessary to make it succeed.

To that end, I enrolled in FIT's fashion and design program, a field in which I felt I could excel. It was time to unleash my creativity. Daddy's lessons on maintaining financial independence were ringing in my ears. I worked while I studied, taking temp jobs as a receptionist to pay my portion of the rent. Titi landed a position as an assistant to the news director at WABC.

You can be short on many things in business and still succeed, but you can't ever be short on passion.

Titi and I were finally coming into our own.

Four

★ ★ ★

YOUNG, GIFTED,
AND BLACK-OWNED

*You seem to be connected to
some universal creative stream.*

—KAREN AKEMI MATSUMOTO (MOM)

I've always had a good sense of when to change gears, and I knew it was time for us to get out of Queens, where things were continuing their downhill slide. For over a year, all Titi and I had been doing was working to pay the rent on a building our father owned in Rockaway, and it wasn't exactly conducive to socializing. It was 1991, and I was going to school at FIT and doing temp jobs all over town while Titi was working in the city. Where we were living required a long commute to the places we needed to be.

Know when it's time to make a change. Be alert to the right moment for making a leap, because nothing holds you back more than clinging to the safety of the status quo.

When I was seventeen, I started hanging out in Brooklyn. I went to a place called Cellars in Clinton Hill a few times. I was exposed to the beauty of the area and could see we were missing out on a whole other life. Something about the place made a lasting impression on me. One morning, over breakfast, I mentioned it to my sister. "Titi, we need to change it up. Most of our friends have moved on, and there's nothing for us here. We need to be in Brooklyn! Those neighborhoods are beautiful. They've got brownstones, tree-lined blocks, and culture."

"You really think that's where we should be? Well, okay, if that's what you want, I'll get us there."

Titi made me feel good because she valued my opinions. When she made a move, it was always based on my input. She would take that direction, then follow through with her own thorough research—the executor of my vision.

A few days after that conversation, my sister arranged for us to look at all kinds of apartments in Brooklyn. We had our hearts set on Fort Greene, which was ground zero for the hip crowd, but the rents were out of our reach. This was good in a way, because once again, it forced us to be a little outside of things—keeping us on the other side of the Flatbush Avenue divide. Our Atlantic Avenue loft was warm, spacious, and inviting, with high ceilings, hardwood floors, and exposed brick walls in every room. Even better, the rent was nine hundred dollars a month, something we could just about afford. Titi occupied the large master bedroom with the walk-in closet, and I slept in the small room to the right. Our father was nice enough to sand and refinish our wood floors, and we furnished it with affordable but stylish IKEA furniture. Adding a few thrift store finds we restored ourselves, we created our first real home—a place that felt like it was truly ours.

WELCOME TO BROOKLYN!

★

We loved our new neighborhood. Brooklyn, in the early phase of its gentrification, was becoming a hive of creativity and entrepreneurship, especially for young African-Americans, with celebrities, media types, and artists calling the streets home. As far as I was concerned, Spike Lee put this community on the map with films like *She's Gotta Have It*, *Do the Right Thing*, and *Mo' Better Blues,* which featured the borough of Brooklyn as a main character and highlighted how beautiful it was. This was a place rich in culture and history that sparked the imagination. Celebrity encounters were typical. In Brooklyn, extraordinary things could happen at any given moment. I even met Mike Tyson while walking my black chow chow, Rheggi Bear. We were in the right place at the right time.

While Queens was the place where we absorbed music influences and honed our street smarts, Brooklyn was the place that refined us, helping us to become more worldly young women. In fact, living in Brooklyn was what prepared Titi and me to brazenly start our own business. The people around us were having a huge impact on how we viewed ourselves, making us realize what was possible. We witnessed the emergence of the gifted black entrepreneur (GBE), including such local talent as Salif Cisse, co-owner of the Senegalese restaurant Keur N'Deye on Fulton Street, hat designer and vendor Ray Hands, and storefront designer Moshood, who specialized in African clothing. Especially noteworthy among this group was Adolmole Mandella, owner of Kinnaps, who not only blazed a trail for natural hair, but also personified the Brooklyn Renaissance. He was one of the first to package this Brooklyn movement of ownership and black pride through branding. We used to see various people walking the streets of Brooklyn in the famous branded black on black leather varsity jacket with the Kinnaps logo emblazoned on the back. It was a wonderful reference point for brand building while creating Miss Jessie's.

These innovators were proud, doing business on their terms. They were repackaging their own culture and making it chic, desirable, and accessible to everyone. Black culture was being commercialized. We loved the fact that they were young, like us, and lived in close proximity. Having peers and neighbors who were such movers and shakers made us feel like we could do it, too.

There was a positive energy to the streets, and that electricity seemed to crackle every time we stepped outside. Besides Mike Tyson, we had popular rappers like Jay-Z, who would drive through the neighborhood in his white four-door Lexus, and Lord Jamar of the hip-hop group Brand Nubian, who lived around the corner on State Street. We also had "Jesse," from the soap opera *All My*

Inspiration is all around you. Believe that if others can do it, you can, too.

Children. They were part of the fabric of the neighborhood. Bohemian Brooklyn was burgeoning, and Titi and I were bumping into all kinds of what we called "BOOMers" (Black-Owned and -Operated Media)—progressive, entrepreneurial, and fearless individuals who gave us something to aspire to. Suddenly, we were mixing it up with this successful, artsy crowd, circulating in the galleries, at poetry readings, and along the shop fronts of this cool section of New York City we now called home.

DOING ME

*

Soon after our relocation, I had an epiphany about what I wanted to do in life: hair.

I'd been searching for the right fit ever since our failed cleaning-business venture with our father. Initially, I made more than a few fumbles. My mother even found me a job in a graphic design shop, which I wasn't feeling. I'd always loved fashion, and I'd inherited my mother's aesthetic sense, so going into fashion seemed like an obvious move.

But mostly, FIT taught me what I didn't want. My courses focused too much on the technical side of the fashion business. I spent long hours in draping and pattern-making class before manually sewing each garment. I'm impatient, and there was no immediate gratification to building a fashion collection. It was a major investment of time and effort, then trying to get financing for it seemed challenging. I quickly figured out it wasn't for me, although I had to finish what I started. Anything to avoid Daddy's usual chastisements if I failed to complete my degree. In the end, that turned out to be a good thing: It helped me to get more focused on my goals. Experiencing the feelings of being on the wrong path motivated me. When I eventually found my way, I benefited from the knowledge I'd gained at FIT. Once I was passionately moving in the right direction, that allowed me to appreciate every single step.

The same day I graduated from FIT, I enrolled in hair school on Thirty-fourth Street in New York City. Although I would never admit it to my parents, I secretly thought I was taking the easy way out and felt a bit guilty, like I was somehow being self-indulgent. I didn't feel like I was challenging myself, because I was naturally good at doing hair. Why did I think my life's work should be a constant grind?

I remembered the thrill it gave me to do my grandmother's hair, and the look of sheer pleasure on her face when she looked at herself in the mirror. That was a gift for me as much as for her. I could spend hours on someone's head and not even notice the passage of time. Purely through the work of my two hands, I could give someone joy, and I wanted to experience that feeling again and again.

Sometimes the right thing is the easiest thing.

Of course, I caught hell for it. This time both my mother and father laughed at my decision. "A hairstylist? Really? Well, I guess you could do celebrity hair to make your career seem more professional," Mommy said. While she'd heard of hair greats, like Vidal Sassoon, she couldn't imagine I would find my creative outlet in hair.

"You'll get varicose veins," Daddy chimed in.

Even though they were divorced by then, our parents were

in agreement on this one thing. Only Titi was supportive. "Miko, don't listen to them. This is something you love, and you are great at it. That's a blessing."

As always, my sister let me do me.

HAIR RAISING

★

Hair school was wild, with all kinds of personalities. There were some sweet, hardworking women, but many were on the rough side, and to call them catty would be an understatement. On a few occasions I witnessed girls come to blows.

One young woman with a long weave like Naomi Campbell's somehow sparked the collective hatred of a group of students. She was attractive, drove a Range Rover, carried an oversize cell phone—which was rare for the early nineties— and was dating a rich Manhattan doctor. One day after class, a group of girls decided to jump her. I stepped out of the building in time to catch the tail end of the scuffle. It got so nasty that one of her attackers pulled that long weave right out of her scalp, forcing the poor woman to flee down the street with bald patches.

My upbringing in Queens had taught me how to defend myself, but I'd also learned how to avoid unnecessary confrontation. I kept my head down and my mouth shut, minding my own business. It was a seven-and-a-half-month course, and all I wanted was to get through it. Again, I couldn't stand the thought of hearing Daddy's rebukes if I failed. But more than that, I wanted to take care of business for my own sake, honing my craft and getting the necessary qualifications to have the career I was meant for. This was a brief stop along the way, a means to an end, and the environment or attitudes of the other students didn't matter. If I'd gotten too involved in the dramas of other people, it would have taken me off my path.

In any case, I didn't have time for distractions. As I was training, I continued to pay the bills by doing full-time hours as a receptionist, and then I started waitressing at a coffee shop in the Village called the Figaro. It wasn't easy work, but those jobs were another aspect of my education, teaching me something about my future business. As a receptionist, I learned how important phone skills can be when handling new clients. The tone of your voice can set the whole mood of the transition. As a waitress, I learned that great service can be integral to a customer's whole experience.

My first job after graduating from hair school in 1994 reinforced those lessons. After being rejected on an interview at Jacques Dessange on Park Avenue in Manhattan, I made my way back to the train station almost in tears. I had not performed well on the hair demo, and I was still stinging from the withering sarcasm of the French hairstylist who'd interviewed me. As I walked along East Sixty-first Street near Bloomingdale's, I spotted an upscale salon—Hair Styling by Joseph—and something told me to walk in. Joe Plaskett, Jr., son of the business's founder and its chief stylist, hired me for an entry-level position right on the spot.

Take care of your clients and treat them with respect.

Discovering Joseph's was eye-opening, because the salon was busy and classy. It was also a family operation that was successful. They'd been in business since 1961, starting from a two-chair salon in the East Village to an establishment that was booked solid every day with VIP clients who came from all over the country to be professionally pampered and groomed. In no time, Joseph's had become the destination for such luminaries as Cicely Tyson, the Ronettes, the Isley Brothers, Patti LaBelle, and Nancy Wilson.

Our experience with our father had jaded us, but here was an example of a business run by the family patriarch, Joseph Plaskett, Sr., in which every member was valued for the role he or she played—the sisters, brothers, in-laws, mother, and father. Years before, they'd bought the multistory town home, each of the three generations occupying a floor, with the lower two levels dedicated to the thriving business. It was a blueprint of how a family business *can* work, and I respected the model.

In some ways, Joseph reminded me of Daddy at his best. He was an entrepreneur at his core who dabbled in all kinds of businesses until one day he announced to his family, "We are going to do hair." He'd come across a number of wealthy and elegant women of color who were lacking a destination salon that could give them top service in an exclusive environment.

At Joseph's, I marveled at all of the women with disposable income. A fair share of professionals, socialites, and celebrities, such as Diana Ross, Tyra Banks, and Angela Bassett, patronized the salon during a time in the early nineties when we were in somewhat of a recession. These VIPs were serviced on the second floor, which was full of A-listers. On some days it looked like the greenroom at the Oscars. But I wasn't starstruck so much as impressed with Joseph's stellar reputation and business savvy. That was my first exposure to the notion that people are willing to pay for quality.

"Wow, Titi, you wouldn't know we were in a recession if you saw all the money these women spend on themselves and their families," I told my sister.

"Really? Hmmm. I guess there must be a level that's recession-proof," Titi said.

"Yes, that, and maybe the fact that when you offer top-quality service, money is no object when it comes to a woman's hair."

> *When you are good at something, you always have something to sell, no matter what is happening in the economy.*

I stayed there for about a year. The salon offered me medical benefits and a guaranteed salary of $250 per week, Tuesday through Saturday, plus tips. I was satisfied and thrilled with my new position. I was actually getting paid to do what I loved. Even better was their willingness to reward hard work and initiative with opportunity.

"Miko, when you first walked into this place, I saw a fire in your eyes," Bryant, a junior stylist at Joseph's, told me. "I could tell you'd do whatever it took to work hard and make it."

Bryant became a fast friend, showing me the ropes and sharing the long train ride back to Brooklyn, where he also lived. According to him, the Plaskett family was extremely picky about whom they would have work in the salon, but they'd welcomed me with open arms. "They knew you were one of them straight away," Bryant teased.

At first, no one wanted me to wash their hair or "get them started for the main stylist." Although that used to hurt my pride, I worked extra hard and volunteered to do everything I could, eventually becoming so proficient that the clients would request and wait for me to prep their hair for the stylist. My relaxer, roller set, and shampoo became impeccable, and I made a point of becoming invaluable to whatever stylist I assisted. This got the attention of the owner, who was affectionately known as "Senior."

Typically, assistants train for one to two years before becoming an assistant, but in a matter of weeks I was assigned to shadow a lovely and talented man named Walter. He taught me a lot, and I admired his good relationships with his clients. Not only was Walter a highly skilled technician, he was focused solely on the satisfaction of his customers, wanting nothing more than for the women who sat in his chair to have a great experience. I took it all in, learning from a master craftsman.

Another stylist I formed a bond with was Kemi. She was Joseph Jr.'s wife, and her name was short for Akemi, my mother's middle name. Kemi was half black and half Japanese, like me, and she was the first woman besides Titi in whom I could see my own mixed-race heritage. She was beautiful, with long, glorious thick hair and a serenity that reminded me of my mother. Kemi seemed to quietly like me. After three months, I got my confidence up and asked her if I could style someone's hair from start to finish. Much to my surprise, she said yes. Within a year of graduating from hair school, I had become a bona fide stylist at one of Manhattan's most exclusive salons. I was always booked, which was unheard of at such a coveted institution.

I loved it at Joseph's. The atmosphere was upscale yet supportive. I felt like part of the family. Of course, the place was strict, with a clear pecking order, and Senior expected us to execute everything perfectly. Although he had retired from doing hair by the time I came, Bryant made sure to let me know the standards set by Senior. "When we prep clients to be seen by the advanced stylist, he doesn't hesitate to make us shampoo their hair all over again if something isn't exactly according to his standards," Bryant shared with me. "Things have to be right when you represent him and his business."

I understood why Joseph was tough. It had to be that way. It was a high-volume business catering to a demanding clientele who expected the best, and an unhappy client never came back. We had to be an extension of that top stylist, acting as his second, third, and fourth pair of hands, to allow each customer to get exactly the same high level of service. It was more information I filed away for future use.

HAIR CATS

★

Finally, I had found my niche, and that gave me professional validation. When I started down this new career path, I did not get too comfortable. An instinct was driving me to try other things, so I went off in search of new techniques at other salons. I wanted to learn as much as I could.

I discovered that the hair business isn't always as friendly as it was in my first salon. I moved on to a trendy shop downtown that attracted younger clients who were into short cuts and weaves—even more celebrity-focused, with hair featured in magazines like *Essence*. I found it a horrible experience.

Maybe, since I was coming from such a nurturing environment, my skin was too thin, but the atmosphere was challenging. At that salon, it wasn't about what the client wanted as much as what the stylist wanted. I found the in-house politics unworthy of the time it would take me to navigate them. I did a few stints at other fancy salons in Manhattan; I had bigger dreams, so I learned what I could and moved on. My dad's constant drumbeat finally took hold. I enjoyed the creative side of hair, as well as the interaction with clients. I wasn't going to let the competitive environment of the salon world distract me from my goals.

Ever the entrepreneur, I increased my expertise in the area where I was born to work: hair and beauty.

HIGHER LEARNING

As I was learning the salon industry across the water in Manhattan, Titi and I dove headlong into the social scene of Brooklyn. We were eager to make as many connections as we could with young black professionals who seemed more sophisticated and worldly than the kids we'd grown up with. In a way, we were completing our education in the school of life, and something told us we could learn from them. Brooklyn was more a university-level education.

One of my professors in this particular life school was Garrett Fortner, author, entrepreneur, and publisher of *New Word Magazine,* a cool grassroots jumbo-sized lifestyle publication focused on the Brooklyn arts scene. It was the first magazine to

put the rapper Lil' Kim on the cover. *New Word* featured everything that was authentic and cool in black culture, with stories
on Spike Lee, Mary J. Blige, and Gary Dourdan, to name a
few. I used to see the larger-than-life magazine covers on news-
stands around the city, and they reminded me that a fresher,
hipper expression of our generation was happening.

I met Garrett in 1996 at an art opening in Brooklyn Moon,
a café on Fulton that was a cool spot for the borough's funky
crowd. It had everything from poetry slams to great sandwiches
and coffee, all in an intimate space reminiscent of an old speakeasy. This tall, extremely slim dude in overalls and an applejack
hat walked right up to me like he owned the place. "Hey, was-
sup, what's your name?" he asked me.

I said nothing, staring and trying to figure out what to
make of the moment. A kind of modern-day Beatnik, he had
Brooklyn written all over him. I came to learn he loved Afrocentric beauty—the blacker, the better. He loved all the things
that made a black woman unique, whether it was the way she
walked, talked, or handled her business. He was black and
proud.

As I got to know him, I learned that Garrett had an authentic Brooklyn demeanor and an entrepreneurial spirit that
intrigued me. He was exactly the kind of person who'd attracted my sister and me to Brooklyn in the first place. Knowing his hands-on grassroots experience in publishing, I figured
he could be a valuable resource. After doing hair on my own for
about nine months, I decided to raise my profile by doing hair
for magazines and other outlets. I thought this would be a good
way to keep new clients coming and to diversify my streams of
income.

When I called Garrett, we arranged to meet up again at the Brooklyn Moon later that day. I wanted to pick his brain some more and learn all I could about how the media world worked. If I was going to become a successful businesswoman, I had to get my name out there. Garrett was quick to make good on his promise and arranged various opportunities for me to do hair, including photo shoots with celebrities like Garcelle Beauvais.

I owe much of what I know about marketing from my long conversations with Garrett, a brilliant entrepreneur who shared many insights on building a business and a brand. It was good to find a mentor besides my father—someone who could give me another perspective to business. Garrett would ask me all sorts of questions to get me to think about my future. He had me map out my career by doing fun exercises, interviewing me like a reporter. As he grilled me, he'd have me spell out three things that I wanted for myself: to own real estate, to have a prosperous family business, and to have a hair product line. Intellectually, he engaged me and got me to focus on things in a way I never had.

Garrett inspired me. Witnessing his world up close was a reminder that there was still a wide gap between where I was in my career and where I wanted to be.

★ ★ ★

Five

READY TO ROLL

You are only as good as your tools.

—JIMMY BRANCH (DADDY)

I started small in my salon business. The point was to keep my overhead as low as possible. I never wanted to be in a position where I couldn't pay my bills. As a result, my business consisted of a chair in our living room. That was all the furniture we had in that space. I had taken my earnings from past jobs to buy a used chair from a salon supply store, and then I took the sink out of our bathroom and replaced it with a shampoo bowl.

It was around this time that my father began to understand how serious I was about a career in hair. To my surprise, he asked me to cut his hair. He wanted a proper men's barber cut—something I had only done once when I was fifteen and cut my high-school friend Ottavio Johnson's hair. I was nervous because I knew Daddy was observing my work, and I was bracing myself for a critique. As I pulled out my cutting tools, trying to get my bearings, I fumbled, nearly dropped the razor, and giggled to cover my embarrassment. In that moment, my father turned around in the chair to face me and told me to switch off the buzz cutter. Then he offered some wisdom: "Miko, you are only as good as your tools. Be in full control when you operate them, and invest in a good set. This is how you can build your craft."

He must have liked my work, because my father, a stickler for good grooming, has trusted me for haircuts ever since. That stamp of approval meant everything.

MAKING RENT

★

My one-chair salon made a small profit, and I was able to cover my part of the bills. However, I did not have a shop front and could not advertise my services on the street. One slow month, it was getting to the point where I couldn't make rent. A friend in the neighborhood told me someone was looking to hire a bartender for a party at the Rose Castle Grand Ballroom in Brooklyn. The woman who ran the catering company, Christine, happened to have a small café around the corner from our apartment, on Fourth Avenue. I stopped by to introduce myself. "Hi, I heard you're looking for someone to work tonight," I told her.

"Ever bartend before?" Christine asked.

"No, but I've waitressed, and I think I can do it," I said, feeling confident.

"Well, all right, you look the part. It pays fifteen dollars an hour, but you get to keep your own tips. How does that sound?"

"That sounds real good, what time?"

I got there early to get a few quick tips on mixing drinks from Christine. We stuck to the basics. If someone ordered something I didn't know how to make, I just had to smile sweetly and offer a rum and Coke or something. It seemed easy enough, because all night almost everyone was ordering Moët or Cristal champagne, no mixing necessary. After the four-hour job, I thought I could make about a hundred dollars with tips and cover my cable and utility bills. I was wrong! I made close to *two thousand* in tips. It turned out to be a huge baller event, with people like that guy who lived around the corner from us on State Street—Jay-Z.

At the end of the shift, Christine came up to me. "Good job, Miko! If you want, you can go home now. The guy has already paid us, and I'm ready to get out of here."

"No, I'm good. I'll keep working until the last guest leaves, if that's okay with you."

I didn't want to leave, because the dollars were still flying at me. It was so much cash that I barely had room in my pocketbook. The night's

> *You have to be willing to do anything, including taking a second job, in order for your business to thrive.*

work enabled me to not only make rent but also to keep my dream alive just long enough to build momentum. Rolling up my sleeves and mixing drinks wasn't beneath me. The experience taught me that a willingness to work hard and learn can carry you through any situation and help further your goal.

GROWING HANDS

★

My first home client was a pretty woman named Sayeda. I started doing her hair while I was still at Joseph's. My plan was to do hair at home as my side hustle until I had a steady base of clients to build a bigger business. I liked to test the waters first.

Titi and I met Sayeda at one of those hipster parties in Harlem that was full of actors, who were among Titi's circle of friends. "Oh my God, I love your hair!" Sayeda gushed at us, then immediately introduced herself. "Are you two sisters? Do you do it yourselves?"

"As a matter of fact, Miko does it for me," said Titi, my biggest cheerleader and unofficial publicist. "She's one of the top stylists in Manhattan."

"Can you do mine?"

Sayeda sat in my chair for twelve hours. Her hair was very thick, and I was not quite at pro status yet, which made me nervous. Over the years, there had been a lot of damage. Years of harsh chemicals and dyes had caused her hair to come out in chunks, by the root—a not-uncommon phenomenon for women of color who put their hair through the wringer in the name of a more European standard of beauty. Sayeda had a chin-length bob that she could never get to grow past her shoulders because of the poor health of her hair roots. Before I cut and styled her hair, I used peppermint oil to soothe her scalp, and I soaked her brittle hair follicles in the richest conditioners I could find on the drugstore shelves.

"You know, Sayeda, you've got to be kinder to your hair. It's a part of you," I told her as we got to know each other in the intimate environment. "Treat it well, and it might actually grow to the length you dream about."

A few months later, Sayeda came back to me with lush, long tresses past her shoulders. "Oh my God, Miko, you have growing hands. My mother said if I wasn't her child, she'd think I was wearing a wig!"

She told everyone she knew, and soon my chair was always busy. All at once I had a business. It was actually working! Not having to work for someone at a nine-to-five job, billing my own clients, making money, and fulfilling my creative side made me feel good about myself for the first time in my life.

Take care of your scalp, and condition hair from tip to root. This is the foundation of beautiful hair.

I was finally coming into my own, hanging out with hip Brooklyn artists and freelancers, sleeping late, and living life on my own terms.

SISTER ACT

---- ★ ----

Never would it have occurred to me that anything I did in business could influence Titi. She was doing well at ABC, filling in for other reporters, conducting interviews, and working as a field producer. My big sister was on track to a promising future. I really admired her for it. But unbeknownst to me, she'd caught the entrepreneurial bug, observing all the small businesses that had started to sprout up in the neighborhood. Titi also saw the freedom I was enjoying as my own boss.

"I handed in my notice today," she told me one day out of the blue.

"What? Why?"

Titi had a way of keeping quiet and brooding on something until she was ready to spring into action.

"There's too much politics in network television. I can't own whatever it is I'm doing, and I'm just not feeling it anymore. I am done."

All along, I had assumed she was happy. Titi was always interested in current affairs. She was knowledgeable, able to communicate even the most complex of ideas persuasively. ABC seemed to be right in her wheelhouse.

Titi caught hell from our family. Miss Jessie simply could not understand why Titi would leave a "good job" at ABC and told her flat out it was a stupid move. "Girl, you're a fool to throw away that good job like that," she scolded, never one to bite her tongue. "If that ain't stupid!"

Daddy, who'd gotten settled with the fact that Titi would not be an entrepreneur and would instead build a career in

the news media, made no secret of the fact that he was annoyed. A daughter who works for a major network news producer comes with plenty of bragging rights, and she'd taken
that away from him.

But I admired her for it. Giving up a job like that took guts.
With no client base to speak of, Titi decided to become an
agent, jumping without a net and determined to build something from nothing.

In 1996 she opened an office on Twelfth Street in the
Village under the name Icon Creative Artists and started representing photographers, using her connections as a producer
and her ingenious way with words to pitch for them. The business wasn't generating any money until Titi started representing me; her passion for my work shone through to prospective
media and advertising outlets. It made perfect sense for the
two of us to get together.

Always one to define everything, Garrett told us: "Miko,
you're the visionary, and Titi is the facilitator, dedicated to your
dream. The two of you together are a powerful force."

He also referred to us as the Delany sisters, after those two
women in Harlem, Bessie and Sadie, who lived together their
whole lives, both well past a hundred. We used to laugh every
time he called us that, but there was something to it. Ever since
we were children, we'd been a great team. By coincidence, our
separate paths were starting to overlap more and more. A lot of
the work Titi was getting for her celebrity photographers came
through some of the top hair salons around New York City. She
also arranged a lot of shoots for hair product companies. When
she got home and we swapped stories about our day, it occurred
to us that we were essentially in the same business.

The fact that my sister was proud of my work and wanted to represent me felt good. I was deeply touched that she placed so much faith in my talent. Titi hustled hard for me, arranging my first photo shoot through a referral she got from a cameraman at ABC. I used my own salon clients and even filled in as a model myself. Titi took care of everything, from the catering (Miss Monique's fried chicken and potato salad) to the delivery of the pictures, reaching out to all the black hair magazines. Adrienne Moore, the editor of *Hype Hair*, one of the hottest hair publications on the market, gave us our very first double-page center spread. Titi's efforts paid off handsomely.

After a robbery at her agency's Village headquarters and months of financial struggle, Titi finally decided to close the doors of that office, relocate her operations to the apartment, and focus entirely on helping me in my career, which was now making money for both of us. I was happy to split my proceeds with her 50/50; I was smitten with the fact that my smart corporate-type sister wanted to represent me exclusively. Titi had to make a move; if not, she would have had to go back to working as someone's employee. The life of an entrepreneur was too good to give up on. That freedom, with no one telling her what to do, must have felt too good. Besides, being an entrepreneur was the new cool. Now Titi just had to make the money to go with the profile. She needed me on board to get her business off the ground.

And soon enough, she did. A wonderful woman, Sonia Alleyne, editor of what was then *Black Elegance* magazine, gave Titi a referral that led to an advertising gig. I did all the models' hair for a print campaign for the Ashley Stewart fashion label, netting us eight thousand dollars—the most money we'd ever seen. It was a perfect example of how our strengths blended together, and confirmation beyond a few satisfied customers in the four walls of my living room that I had something. People in the advertising and fashion industries recognized that I was doing good work, and that meant the world to me.

BREAKING OUT

★

While I was enjoying a private moment in between hair appointments, Titi burst into my room."Miko, we are going to open a salon."

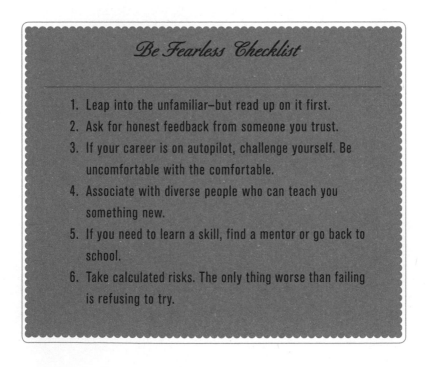

Be Fearless Checklist

1. Leap into the unfamiliar–but read up on it first.
2. Ask for honest feedback from someone you trust.
3. If your career is on autopilot, challenge yourself. Be uncomfortable with the comfortable.
4. Associate with diverse people who can teach you something new.
5. If you need to learn a skill, find a mentor or go back to school.
6. Take calculated risks. The only thing worse than failing is refusing to try.

As unexpected as it was, taking our partnership to the next level made perfect sense. Knowing me better than anyone else, she realized I needed that extra nudge. You've got to stretch to grow, but sometimes I felt too safe and cozy in my own little space to want to move. The thought of having to cover a higher overhead was terrifying. Titi was pushing me to take a risk and step out of my comfort zone. I wanted more, but I believed I was already doing something big with a few clients a day to cover my life expenses, with a little extra as disposable money. I was loving the freedom to have fun. The idea of leaving the house scared me.

Titi's insistence pushed me out of my own way. I went along with my sister because she was so insistent. We looked all over downtown Brooklyn and even considered a spot that was thirty-five hundred dollars a month. Garrett was highly upset when I told him the asking rent. "That would be a stupid move," he told us. "Make the money first before you put that kind of pressure on yourselves."

In the spring of 1997, Titi found the perfect spot—a small two-chair salon at 103 Bond Street in Boerum Hill, Brooklyn. She marched me up Atlantic Avenue, three lights up from our loft, and pointed to this cute, leafy area around the corner that almost looked like a village, with brownstones, or what the locals call "row houses," and a couple of boutiques nearby. It was mostly residential, but there was plenty of traffic going by, and the place felt safe.

Okay, I thought, drawing in a deep breath. *I can do this.*

At Garrett's suggestion, we called the place Curve, a cool and simple name that suggested something feminine and different from the norm. After all, we were never those "straight line" kind of girls.

Curve was the first salon of its kind in Brooklyn. Its decor was eclectic, warm, and inviting. We used the revenue from the Ashley Stewart campaign as seed money, which just about covered our up-front costs for rent, renovations, and furnishings. We did it all on a budget, with a little help from our mother, who had a great eye for interior design. On a mission to give the place some style, Titi hunted the thrift shops, where she found a set of four retro burgundy leather swivel chairs made out of beer barrels for a hundred dollars. We restored and converted them into salon dryers.

Use What You've Got to Start Any Business

1. If you don't have the capital, use your contacts.
2. Homeownership is another resource, because it's possible to start something out of your own living room or basement.
3. Hard work and creativity—not to mention your own God-given talent—are assets that can be part of the foundation of your start-up.

Whatever the business you hope to launch, use all that you've got. Once you really start looking, you'll find you possess more assets than you ever realized.

Using the renovation skills we'd honed as children when Daddy was selling properties, Titi and I spent the first month after we signed the lease sanding and staining the floors a red mahogany. We worked within our tight budget, shopping at Home Depot and learning what we had to do. Our mother, who was thrilled to help, used her artistic skills to do an amber-and-gold-glazed brushed wall treatment behind the dryer chairs to make them stand out.

All this activity—hammering, sanding, and painting—attracted the attention of Victor, a guy with a distinct Harlem flair. Even though Victor lived uptown, we already knew him from the neighborhood because he worked across the street from our apartment on Atlantic Avenue as an X-ray technician. Although he was around our age, he was fast-talking and worldly, an old soul with a lot of wisdom to share. It felt good to have a man we could trust close by. Victor was always looking out for us and offering ideas. For all his rough edges, he had his own creative side, with a passion for photography and rare art objects. Anyone we attracted into our orbit seemed to have this artistic streak.

He was thrilled when he saw what we were up to, always ready to lend a hand putting up shelves or doing some heavy lifting. "Y'all amaze me," he told us one day when he was hanging out in our shop on his coffee break. "I can't believe the two of you sanded these floors with that heavy industrial sanding machine. And you stained them with this fly-ass burgundy color, too?"

"Sure, Victor. Who else is going to do it if we don't do it ourselves?" Titi replied.

"What's so amazing about that?" I asked him.

"Back in Harlem, most women with your beauty would be living and eating off their looks," he said. "Not you two! Y'all are working hard to pursue your dreams. That's what I love to see!"

It was coming together. By the time we were finished, Curve looked more like a hip, cozy living room and less like a typical salon, filled with plants, bunches of fresh-cut flowers we bought at the Korean market, and comfortable chairs. It was a combination of the Southern hospitality we'd learned from Miss Jessie, and the elegant aesthetic we'd picked up from our mother, who always knew exactly where to place a chair or drape a fabric. Visually, it stood out, especially from the street, because it had a huge glass picture window with two styling stations lit by the kind of lightbulbs typical of an old Hollywood movie set.

Even then, we were our cheapest and best hair models. Titi got one of the photographers she'd been representing to do a professional photo session at a deep discount. A portrait of us with healthy hair stood front and center in the salon window. People were compelled to stop and look. There was even a stop-light on the corner of Bond Street and Atlantic Avenue that held cars in front of our salon.

All eyes were on us, and before long, the place was jumping. But I still didn't have peace of mind. It upset me that Titi had pushed me to jump in with both feet while she was maintaining a part-time job at Citibank's headquarters—a gig she'd taken as backup. I understood why. We had to be certain we could pay the rent. But being in the salon by myself terrified me. I had never been that exposed to the public, and I needed my sister there with me. It was time for her to be all the way in.

"Titi, I can't be in the salon alone all day," I told her. "You never know who's going to come in off the street. It's not safe for me! You need to be there, too."

Realizing that the gig could be up if I bailed, Titi decided to join me at the salon full-time. Soon we became known as "the two girls with the cute salon."

TAG TEAM

★

Even though most of our business revolved around hair straightening (I did a damn good relaxer), we wanted the salon to become known as the go-to place for healthy hair. With my early training at Hair Styling by Joseph, mixed with other techniques I'd learned along the way, I'd become a well-rounded stylist and had complete confidence in my craft. After seeing all the damage that women were doing to their hair, I felt the emphasis had to be on conditioning and counterbalancing the harsh effects of chemical relaxers. The focus paid off, and we made a profit within the first month of business. We were both excited!

At first Titi supported me in the business by taking calls, greeting customers, handling marketing, and administering payroll; she did all the grunt work restoring, maintaining, and cleaning the premises. Beyond that, she brought some business sense. My book was always full for the simple reason that my brilliant sister asked our satisfied customers when they wanted to make their next appointment. As a one-woman show in our studio apartment, I never thought to rebook a client; I had to wait until my clients called me. That one small change in ap-proach had a huge impact, improving cash flow, leaving less to chance, and making my schedule much more predictable and easy to manage.

Get a partner, but choose wisely. Two heads can be better than one, as long as you have a clear understanding of who does what the best.

Titi had a way with the customers, perfectly articulating the process for them with a quick informal consultation before they had the actual hair service. She'd examine the condition of their hair and make follow-up suggestions to help them improve their hair health and maintain their look long after they left the salon. It was all part of the rotation, which prevented clients from feeling like they were sitting around untended to. Unlike the beauty shop experience, where women might wait around for hours before seeing a stylist, our system moved them through our chairs as quickly as possible. We did not want to waste their valuable time. What wait time they did have, we wanted to be a pleasurable experience, so we always played music and offered good, wholesome conversation to give our ladies the sense that they were having a fun day at the salon. This approach helped us create a steady stream of great customers. It was a little of Miss Jessie coming through. She never let anyone step through her door without acknowledgment.

Meanwhile, I was happy to do every single head of hair that came through the door. Oftentimes it was a twelve-hour day, and we worked typical salon days, from Tuesday until Saturday.

I was getting a workout, but I could not think of anything I'd rather do.

Titi couldn't do hair at first, but she learned as she went, starting by giving the best shampoos. Our customers used to look forward to seeing Titi at the sink, because she started with a soothing scalp massage. That was smart, because destressing our clients with a head massage and extra pampering made my job easier. They would emerge from the shampoo bowl feeling relaxed and more receptive to my styling suggestions.

One thing about Titi I admired was that whenever she didn't know something, she didn't hesitate to research a topic. She was a quick study, carefully watching how I handled the process of cutting and styling, taking a few courses of her own, eventually graduating to occasional styling. It was almost as if she had been to beauty school; she was assisting me the same way I assisted Walter at Joseph's. Now there were two of us carrying the load, and that enabled us to double our volume.

Overall, Titi brought a fresh perspective to the beauty business. Her gift with people and her desire to foster long-term relationships with customers gave us a huge advantage. She wasn't simply focused on the immediate return. She was building something. Her organizational and planning skills gave our tiny salon a professional patina that built confidence in the women who walked through our door.

On many levels, we had the perfect combination of talent and business-mindedness. My sister had an innate ability to know when to pitch in and do what was needed, leaving me to focus exclusively on our clients and their hair. I didn't even have to say anything. She read my mind.

By handling all of the other aspects of our business, Titi

allowed me to truly excel at my craft. She created an environment for me that was free of all of the politics and pitfalls of the
salon and beauty industry. I looked at my sister as a savior of
sorts, because without her influence, I might never have taken
my career and our business to a whole other level. I was both
happy and grateful. We were winning—together.

* * *

HARD PRESSED

Business was steady to the point where we were banking 50 percent of our earnings and using the rest to operate our salon. Our overhead was low because we were still living together and sharing everything, even our clothes, allowing us to amass a good amount in our savings account. Knowing that we were covered gave us a sense of security and well-being we'd never experienced.

Titi and I were doing it all side by side, building the family business we'd dreamed about since the days we were locked in the backseat of our father's Chevy, waiting for him to close on a deal.

It was a warm morning in April, and I was looking forward to a full day of bookings at our salon when Titi, who'd stayed out the night, pulled up in front of the apartment in her red stick-shift Acura to take us to work. As soon as I climbed in the passenger seat, I noticed the look on her face. Something was seriously wrong.

Pool your resources whenever possible. Doubling up saves money that can be put into the bank, or back into the business when necessary.

"Miko, I have to tell you something," she said in a way that made me think someone had died.

"Oh my God, Titi! What's wrong?"

"We owe the IRS a lot."

My stomach lurched. After a little over a year in business, we'd allowed ourselves to think of our revenues as profits. It never occurred to us to do the math and figure out what we owed Uncle Sam off the top. Besides, our earnings had been subsistence-level for so long that we were used to getting money *back* from the IRS, not the other way around.

"How much, Titi?" I asked, barely able to breathe. "Wha . . . what's the damage?"

"Seventeen thousand."

We had never seen a bill like that, much less paid one. But there was no way out; we had to cut a check. We were both clear that you don't mess with the IRS.

Our upbringing had taught us to be frugal, so we had the money in our account to cover it, but we weren't as far ahead as we thought we were. In a way, it felt like all the work we'd been doing the previous year was to pay the government. But in that moment I knew exactly what to do. Things were going to be different the next tax year.

"We have to buy something, now," I told Titi. "If we're going to sink our money into something, it might as well be a roof and four walls."

My credit was bad by this time. I'd overspent while at college and did not have the discipline or income to pay back a student credit card. Many young people get stuck with debt after getting their first credit cards. But Titi's credit was good, so it was an easy decision.

We had enough savings to cover a down payment. Titi did her usual deep dive into the research and started looking for property immediately, to enable us to be in a position to write off something that tax year. But as Titi discovered, the prices in downtown Brooklyn were out of our league in 1998. A place in one of the less affluent areas of Brooklyn was all we could afford. Once I understood where the market was, and exactly what we had to work with in our budget, I knew I wanted a brownstone in the Bedford-Stuyvesant section of Brooklyn. Although we'd always stayed close to the center of things, downtown, my friend Christine—the one who got me the bartending job—had invited me to her block party on Hancock Street the year before, and that memory had stayed with me.

I was completely taken with the Old World charm of that

> *Always plan for taxes. Set enough aside, and put your income to work for you through legitimate investments in and outside of the business.*

particular street, with its grand Victorian brownstones and a line of mature oak trees planted in front of each stoop. Scattered in between the rough areas of Bed-Stuy were several blocks that looked like a stately village out of a time capsule. The turrets, cornices, columns, and arches of their nineteenth-century facades had been lovingly preserved over the generations, and reminded me of the romance of a European city—nothing like what we were used to seeing in Queens. I had never forgotten how majestic these pockets seemed, with the rust-red, brown, and terra-cotta rows of houses that glowed a fiery orange as the setting sun hit their stone fronts. It looked like a majestic village built for kings and queens. I know beauty when I see it, and I envisioned us owning property on that exact street. Mind you, that was all I had seen of Bed-Stuy.

Working on my behalf, as always, Titi left me in our crowded salon on a Saturday to go to an open house she found in *The Daily News* for a brownstone on that exact block: Hancock Street, asking price $235,000. There were thirty people at the open house, but Titi eventually scored the property for us by calling the owner every day. It quickly turned into a teacher-student exchange when she confided that she had never bought property. She called that man a million times with questions, and he was happy to oblige. They wanted out of the property, and Titi let it be known that she was a serious buyer. Once the dialogue was established by my sister—the good cop—I stepped in and became the bad cop, negotiating the price down to $215,000. Again, we made the perfect tag team. In July 1999, our father attended the closing with us, and we could sense that he was proud. Now we owned a business *and* a home. "Do or die, Bed-Stuy, here we come!"

WHAT'S GOING ON?

——————————————————— ⋆ ———————————————————

But here's the thing about success—you can never assume it's going to continue. An entrepreneur's life is complex and full of moving parts that include both the personal and the professional, especially when family is involved. Just when things seem to be going well, other pieces can fall out of sync. Working hard every day to expand the bottom line can lead to neglecting your happiness and a healthy life balance. It can lead to bad decision-making.

Around two years into business, right after we closed on the house on Hancock Street, Titi started pushing for us to make another move. I didn't understand the urgency. Things were going well where we were. But Titi had larger ambitions. She shared that because we'd experienced such immediate success with the original salon, we could do it again. "Miko, we can't even take fifteen clients at a time," she argued. "At two hundred and fifty square feet, we're busting at the seams!"

In 1999 Titi talked me into expanding Curve again, two blocks up on Bond Street, to a space that was five times larger than our original 250-foot salon at 103 Bond Street. Before I had time to consider the move, she presented me with a lease.

"Don't we need a lawyer to look at this?" I asked her.

"No, we do not, Miko. You're so paranoid. No one checks every single thing. That's not how business is done."

That's what can happen in a family business. There is a familiarity that can all too easily lead to the dismissal of a valid concern. In a regular partnership, my objections would have been taken more seriously. But we were in the thick of our big sister/ little sister dynamic, and it hurt the decision-making process.

On some level, I could see Titi's logic. She saw how booked out we always were, and identified an opportunity to expand. As a businesswoman, she believed our next step was to grow in capacity, spreading out in stages until, who knew, we could become our own version of Vidal Sassoon or the Regis salons. The problem was, we'd been in business less than two years.

LOCATION, LOCATION

★

We made the classic mistake of many entrepreneurs who, flush with their first success, get overly ambitious and expand too much, too soon, overlooking some key details. We made several rookie errors.

Miss Jessie warned us we were making a stupid move. She was on the phone all the time, blasting my sister for her bad judgment. "Titi, you had no business being that reckless," she told her. "You're moving too fast, and it's costing too much."

We hadn't done the proper research. For starters, the new place on the corner of State Street and Bond Street was far too big, so the salon appeared half empty, which is never a good look. Those fifteen people who made the first salon look like it was busting at the seams did very little to make the second location look full. When choosing a location, especially in a place like Brooklyn, where a charming neighborhood can turn sketchy over a single block, one move can make or break you.

The space was cute enough, although it had a more commercial, less personal feel. But the location, just two blocks away and on the other side of Atlantic Avenue, was seedy. Nearby were empty lots, a pawnshop, and a homeless shelter. Gone were the trees and cute row houses. There was only one working street lamp on the block, leaving passersby feeling vulnerable, as if any minute someone might jump out and mug them in the darkness. It meant our existing clientele no longer felt safe making the journey to our new salon. As a result, we lost business.

The lease also had a few holes in it, leaving us at a significant disadvantage. Our landlord felt our rent was too low and was eager to drive us out, so he stuck it to us. He withheld our hot water and cut off the heat in the middle of winter. We were

Look-Before-You-Leap Checklist

1. Dive deep into the research before you expand.
2. Consider all the possible issues that could negate the benefit of larger capacity.
3. Do a reality check on the present state of business for a realistic picture of future growth.
4. Enter through that new door with your eyes wide open.

doing hair in our coats! Of course, we protested, but he defied us to battle him in landlord-tenant court. It was exhausting and demoralizing.

Not that we had any intention of giving up. To fill the salon with bodies and create at least the appearance of success, Titi insisted we start offering discount rates—ten- and five-dollar wash-and-sets. I was working double time now. We could no longer afford an assistant, and it fell to Titi to put out the fires. There were plenty to keep her busy. The police came to our salon just about every other day in response to our ongoing disputes with the landlord, scaring away yet more clients. We lost a chunk of our savings, most of our customer base, and to top it off, my belly was swelling with a pregnancy. I had just broken up with my long-term boyfriend but decided to keep the baby, even if that meant raising him on my own. I was frightened for myself and my unborn child.

In between appointments, I used to gaze out our windows at a new shop across the street from us called Polish. It was a nail salon, but not like any other I had seen. It was a one-to-three-operator business with the owner, Erika Kirkland, doing services herself. She even had celebrities like Star Jones, and many magazine editors, making the trek to our sketchy block, getting herself flattering write-ups in the press. Erika had some experience working with Bliss spas, and she'd learned a thing or two from the high-end chain. She required customers to make a deposit to secure an appointment. If they canceled, they forfeited their money to cover her time and loss of potential income. As we were drowning on the other side of the street, I became fascinated with Erika's business methods and filed away what I observed.

OH YES, IT'S PERSONAL

★

Not that there was much time to act on this new intelligence. I gave all I had to keep our business alive, working my tail off. But it was becoming clearer by the day that we were on life support. In a matter of months, I'd gone from what I thought was the perfect life to this. It made me angry. People say it's not personal, it's business, but for me, business is *always* personal. It's an extension of who I am, and when everything I've worked hard for comes under attack, it feels like a violation of my very being. I'd done everything Titi had asked of me and allowed her to make decisions for both of us. The situation was similar to the one that I'd permitted to happen with my father when we were running Branch Cleaning Agency. My gut told me it was wrong, and I didn't listen.

My business-wise sister put everything we'd built at risk. I was far more inclined to resent her for it because she was family. But the mistake we had made was fairly typical of small-business owners.

Miss Jessie was no fan of mine during this period. While she was disappointed in Titi for taking us in the wrong direction, she told me: "There's no need to be hateful to your sister. Your attitude will only make things worse."

Things went further south, and the tension between my sister and me went on for the duration of my pregnancy. Most business partners would be able to go to their individual homes and have some time and

Pace your growth to make sure it is sustainable. Many businesses fail when they expand too rapidly.

distance, but we had no money for separate abodes. We were right on top of each other 24/7: in the house, always aware of the other's presence creaking up the old wooden staircase; in the car, driving past a barren, treeless wasteland of burned-out lots and storefronts on the way to work.

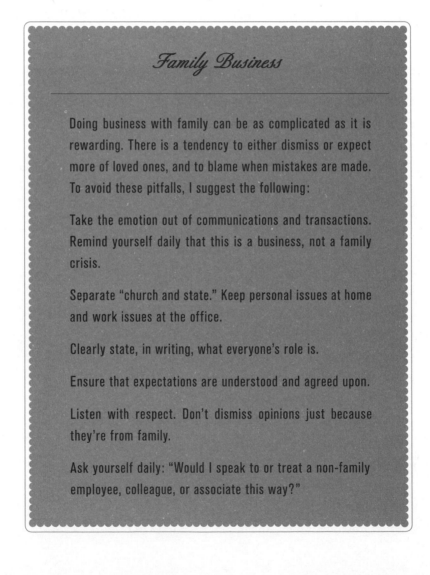

Family Business

Doing business with family can be as complicated as it is rewarding. There is a tendency to either dismiss or expect more of loved ones, and to blame when mistakes are made. To avoid these pitfalls, I suggest the following:

Take the emotion out of communications and transactions. Remind yourself daily that this is a business, not a family crisis.

Separate "church and state." Keep personal issues at home and work issues at the office.

Clearly state, in writing, what everyone's role is.

Ensure that expectations are understood and agreed upon.

Listen with respect. Don't dismiss opinions just because they're from family.

Ask yourself daily: "Would I speak to or treat a non-family employee, colleague, or associate this way?"

I was also disappointed by the father of my child, who made it perfectly clear as the months rolled on that he wasn't going to step up. I didn't want to become one of those welfare mothers Daddy used to hold up to me as a warning for "where pretty gets you." It was up to me to survive.

GRAND OLD LADY

★

Although getting back into the workforce and doing a nine-to-five was not an option for my sister, Titi went about silently trying to fix things in the house. She took a course on home renovation to at least help make our new home in Bed-Stuy more livable. There was a great deal to do, because the previous owners hadn't done any renovations in generations. It was evident that the property had been kept strictly for investment purposes. Besides the basic cosmetics of painting walls and finishing floors on all five stories, we had to upgrade all the electricity and plumbing on a shoestring budget. It was a lot of work for one person, but she never complained.

Physically, I was limited as to how much I could help my sister. My pregnancy, which hadn't been easy, precluded any heavy lifting. While I concentrated exclusively on styling hair, doing as many customers as I could while my ankles and fingers swelled and my back ached, Titi did everything else. For months, she went back to the menial labor she was doing from the very beginning, sweeping, shampooing, answering phones.

We quickly came to terms with reality and cut our expenses down to the bone. After six months of trying, we gave up the Bond Street lease and moved the business into the living room on the parlor floor of the brownstone we'd purchased in Bed-Stuy. It had to be a quick evacuation, as we scrambled to borrow a friend's truck and enlisted Victor's help in loading all our equipment and belongings. Then there were more renovations to hook up the sinks and get the place ready for clients. Until then, every day that passed represented a significant loss of income.

With nothing but hard work, determination, and some nasty chemicals she picked up at the hardware store, Titi stripped away sixty years' worth of paint and wallpaper to reveal beautiful original details. As it turned out, our house in the 'hood was a grand and graceful old lady, radiating character from every corner. Pulling away old carpeting, we discovered perfectly preserved parquet flooring, which Titi sanded and refinished. Inch by inch, Titi was uncovering a treasure. On the sills, door frames, and pilasters, we discovered stunning wood moldings with incised lotus and vine designs in the Eastlake ornamental style typical of the period when the home was built, in 1910 (yes, Titi researched it all when we moved in). All this fine detail was featured on the original sliding French doors that divided the parlor in two, making it an ideal setting for our home salon.

We used the front half for the waiting area and located our sinks and styling stations on the garden side, beyond the French doors. When Titi was through with her handiwork and we'd reinstalled all of our salon equipment from Bond Street,

No task is too small. Pitch in and do whatever needs to be done to keep costs down and to sustain and grow what is yours.

including the Hollywood bulb mirrors, the place was transformed. We used everything we had and invested every dollar
we made into this single floor of the house, to the point where
it had become a kind of oasis in the middle of Bed-Stuy. As one
of my clients would observe years later, "It's like some 1930s
parlor in Harlem where all the beautiful jazz singers would go
to do their hair." That was exactly what we were going for.

As soon as the place was ready, we proceeded to try to
build the business back up from scratch.

A BRAND-NEW WAVE

★

This time it would be different. I was done with the wash,
set, and blowout specials. The Dominicans were already en-
croaching on our market, straightening hair at cut-rate prices.
Discounting my services made me feel cheap and depleted my
soul. I felt every blow, because I was doing all the work. The
cheap prices also made little sense when we factored in labor
and expenses and our low volume of customers. There was no
way anyone but a handful of diehard regulars would make the
trip to Hancock Street. Most of our regulars got turned off over
the phone. When they called to find out where we'd moved to,
this is how the conversation would go:

"Hancock Street! Where's that?"

"Oh, it's easy. You just take the A train to Nostrand Avenue."

"Where? What neighborhood is that?"

"Bed-Stuy."

"Oh, okay, I'll call you back."

We got a lot of that, although some callers were more direct about it:

"What the hell you doing all the way out there?" was one reaction.

"Say what? Take the A train to Nostrand Avenue? Are you crazy?" was another.

People just didn't want to make the journey past the corner bodegas with dudes standing out front, loud street vendors, pawnshops, public housing, and vacant lots. Clients had to really want to see us to be willing to walk past some of the blocks that got you to our little haven on Hancock. This meant that our salon had to become a destination spot—a place where clients could get something that was impossible to find anywhere else. It was time for a total reinvention: new rules, new techniques, new pricing, and a brand-new market. Looking back past all the initial trauma, forcing ourselves to make a fresh start, was probably for the best. We had nothing to lose, because hardly anyone was coming to us.

TAKING CONTROL

In mid-May 2000, my son, Faison, was born. There was no time to heal. I had bills to pay and mouths to feed. In many ways, that was a good thing, because it gave me clarity. Sometimes you make the best decisions when your back is up against the wall.

Fortunately, to make up for those years of absence, our mother gave up her life in Zen retreat for my sake. I was shocked, as she had never said no to those people.

"It is an opportunity to help you as a single mother, and an unrepeatable, wonderful opportunity to be a part of Faison's first year of life," Mommy told me. "I am so grateful for this."

For the first year of my son's life, she moved in with us, helping me out with the day-to-day child care and allowing me to focus exclusively on my craft. I gave her some money to cover her expenses, but her presence was priceless. It was a lifesaving intervention at a time when I couldn't afford a nanny. My mother made fresh squash, carrots, and pureed bananas for my growing boy and healthy, nutritious meals for me. She was always careful with the timing of her cooking and movements inside the house, to keep the atmosphere in the salon more professional than domestic. Her nurturing presence rehabilitated me.

That year went by fast, and when it was over, Mommy left for Japan to continue her training as a Zen nun. I was on my own again, juggling work with the care of my baby boy.

A NEW LOOK

Tending to the needs of my little boy made a woman out of me. One evening during Faison's bath time, an idea came to me. When I put him in the sudsy water, he was a slippery bundle of squealing delight who generated a surprising amount of power while he splashed and shook his tiny fists. All that giggling and wriggling was the highlight of my day, but it left me and my hair a soaking-wet mess. This was not good, because it took me hours to get my thick hair straightened and styled to perfection. I'm a hairstylist with a reputation for making my clients look as if they've just stepped off a magazine cover, so I have a personal standard of grooming to uphold. It was not an option to pull my hair back, give in to the frizz, or wear it under a hat.

It wasn't like I could just start all over: I had to wash, condition, roll, set, sit under the dryer, and then blow my hair out straight. The goal of all this effort was to produce long, silky tresses that resembled European women's hair—a next-to-impossible aesthetic standard for women of color that's existed for generations. To maintain that ironed-out look, it typically takes at least one salon visit a week, which might be dragged out over hours if you include wait time.

Since giving birth, I'd been slowly moving away from that highly coiffed version of perfection. It was a gradual change as I experimented with curly looks and grew out some of the relaxer, but it was subtle, and the result wasn't quite working for me. I felt like a work in progress.

Physically and mentally, I'd been feeling overwhelmed, and it was time to take back control. It was time to shed my old skin and come up with a whole new look. It was also necessary to figure out a way to appear polished and fresh without having to go through my weekly and daily straightening rituals.

Turn crisis into opportunity. There's no better time to take a risk than when you have nothing to lose.

As I stood in front of my bathroom mirror, I decided to take some drastic action.

When I came downstairs to our salon on the second floor, Titi took one look at me and flipped. "Miko," she gasped, "what are you doing?"

Through the magic of a needle, thread, and curly brown and blond weave hair, I'd gone from a Kimora Lee Simmons look—dark shoulder-length hair with a soft bend at the ends—to a wild head of tight and loose curls. I had been watching a lot of television at the time, and I really loved Free's blond Afro on Black Entertainment Television's *106 & Park*. In the late nineties, while most personalities I saw on television sported straight hair, Free rocked her natural 'fro with style.

I loved my new look, but to judge by my sister's reaction, you'd think I'd inked a tattoo on my face. "What's the problem? You don't like it?" I asked Titi, mildly amused. If she only knew I'd been thinking about dyeing my hair blue and getting a nose ring. I felt like the teenage girl in Queens again, going left when everyone else was going right, and it gave me such joy.

"You're going to ruin our business!" she shrieked.

Titi was afraid that, as the face of and the head of the hair salon we ran, I was going to scare away our clients. But I knew in my bones that it was time to take over and do something bold. I was thinking of a master plan.

I could no longer afford to allow anyone to be in control of my failures or successes. Throughout most of my life, I had been passive, letting others make, and take responsibility for, the hardest decisions. I was the artist leaving everyone else to tend to practical matters while I focused on the vocation I loved. But that's no way to run a business or a life. I could not blame anyone but myself if I did not take 100 percent responsibility for my own life.

Treat your business as you would your own child. Protect and nurture it.

GAME CHANGERS

★

Changing up my hair was not just an act of self-expression; it was my moment of insight. Instead of allowing others to be in control, then going with the flow, I was going to do what worked for me and my son. Motherhood had sharpened my focus. Faison helped me to understand that it was no longer just about me and my creative passion. I was a businesswoman with bills to pay, and having that tiny being depend on me was all the motivation I needed to start paying attention to all aspects of our business. As a result, I was charging ahead, trusting my gut, and doing whatever was necessary to feed my baby. That meant some bold changes, including a whole new way of doing hair, not just for myself but for our clients. From now on, we were going to specialize in curls!

I'd already started doing cuts and treatments catering to this market. In 1999, right before we moved out of 71 Bond Street, Titi sent out a press release that included our last photo shoot. The move had gotten us a write-up in *Time Out New York*, which wanted to feature me as a curl specialist. The article encouraged a handful of women, mostly white, to make the trip to the 'hood to find me. We'd lost many of our original customers after moving into our brownstone, but the new customers followed us. It was a burst of activity that generated just enough income to tide us over during one of the worst periods in our business.

Initially, we were surprised by this new customer, but we were also excited. It gave me the opportunity to work with a multitude of curly-hair types, and it was a pleasant departure from all the hair straightening that had been my bread and butter until that point. The more familiar I became with the intricacies of each hair type, the more I thought about what I could do for women with a tighter-coiled curl.

That wave of business from outside the community also meant there was a large untapped market. I realized that many black women could benefit from my updated hair techniques. It was just a question of becoming more proactive in reaching this customer and making her aware that we had the expertise to work wonders with her God-given hair texture.

For too long, natural hair was called "nappy"—an insult to all of us and the very worst thing you could say about our hair. I wanted to show the world that it wasn't nappy, it was curly. For the most part, hair services put women in two categories: overprocessed and stick-straight, or all-natural. Women had become distant from their roots, literally and figuratively. They had no idea that beautiful, shiny, defined curls were possible. As a result, there was no happy medium, and I could sense the frustration in many of my existing clients. My gut told me there had to be countless women who wanted what I had already given myself.

This required drastic action. I decided we were going to do what no one else could do: make a black woman's natural hair texture look great by focusing on the texture and curl pattern. From now on, I was going to use all the skills I'd been honing to give her gorgeous curls and free her from those weekly salon visits that often took hours. Who had time for that? Today's woman wanted to spend her time doing what she enjoyed. Times were changing. She wanted to get up off of that salon chair so she could live her life and pay her bills.

In short, her wants and needs were no different from my own.

Allowing my hair to go curly felt freeing, and I wanted nothing more than to spread that joy. I would use both natural and chemical methods to give her what she wanted. In other words, whatever worked for me would surely work for thousands of other working moms and professional women. This option was missing in the marketplace.

My instincts were right. Within a year, our phone was constantly ringing with women willing to fly in from all over the country. Within two years, we were earning $300,000 to $400,000 a year, one of our early milestones; we were making $700,000 in revenues annually and gaining a national reputation as leaders of the natural-hair movement, right from our brownstone in Bed-Stuy, Brooklyn.

Seven

* * *

IT'S ALL ABOUT THE HAIR

You'll tell two friends, and they'll tell two friends, and so on, and so on, and so on . . .

—FABERGÉ ORGANICS SHAMPOO COMMERCIAL, CIRCA 1980

Mapping out what needed to be done with my client's hair, with its tight, almost impenetrable kink in the back and crown area and a typical looser kink in the front, I was so focused on its intricacy and texture that I almost didn't hear her at first.

"Why are you charging me so much for this?" she repeated, a little louder this time. "None of the other salons are this expensive. What makes you so special?"

I looked up to see a pair of angry eyes flashing at me in the mirror. This lady was not pleased with me, and she was determined to make her point. In 2002 she'd paid the twenty-five-dollar nonrefundable deposit, fully aware of what I charged for my services, and made the trip all the way from downtown Brooklyn to our home salon in Bed-Stuy, so she clearly wanted what I had to offer, regardless of the price I was charging. It happened time and again with our natural-hair customers, especially in the early days of our business.

"You know, a hundred and twenty-five dollars isn't all that much when you think about it," I told her. "I'm going to spend the next three to four hours washing, combing, parting, detangling, cutting, blow-drying, and natural-styling your hair manually. You're going to walk out of here with a lustrous head of curls that you didn't even know was possible. And I'm going to give you all the information you need to keep it looking this good. You will have this knowledge for the rest of your life. Matter of fact, you may not need a stylist after I share my techniques with you."

Our customers typically spent a minimum of twenty-five or thirty dollars at other salons, where they were beholden to their stylists for weekly straightening and blowouts. That added up to at least three hundred dollars in the period between salon visits. Not to mention the time investment—up to a full day in the salon, mostly waiting around, depending on how busy the salon was. Titi did a good job of patiently explaining before they came in, but occasionally, a customer would feel like she had to test me as I was doing her hair.

After I explained the process to her and why it cost what it did, the woman zoned out while I went to work transforming her kinky, tight, and coarse hair, elongating each strand to create a crowning glory of defined, touchable, moisturized, springy curls. By the end of the process, she looked beautiful, with a brand-new head of curls. When she peered in the mirror, she gave me a sheepish smile. "Is this really my hair, Miko? Is my hair really naturally curly? I have had this hair for over forty years! I never knew it could be this different and nice. I have curls."

Of course, she came back.

Sometimes it's necessary to educate your customer. It was only later on, typically a month or two after the first salon visit, that they finally understood the full value of their investment. Titi and I were empowering them with the tips they needed to live their lives and keep themselves looking good until I saw them again. I was

Know your worth. Yes, you can charge a premium when you're offering a unique service or product. Customers will pay for value.

giving them freedom *and* saving them money in the long run.

Internet chat rooms helped with this education process. We focused on teaching, sharing the secrets of proper hair and scalp care, and dispelling some of the misinformation about natural hair. One of the main myths was that natural hair is easier to style and maintain than relaxed hair. That's not necessarily true. It takes care, conditioning, and effort to maintain a healthy, gorgeous head of natural curls. Yes, some mornings you can just get up and go, but most of the time it needs tending with products and techniques like the double strand twist, in which two small sections of hair are twisted together (more on these techniques at the end of the book). Unless women go for short barber cuts, or what we call "The Big Chop," which can limit styling options, natural hair has so much more volume that it requires a lot of time. It helped women to know that they would need to be involved in their own hair maintenance before they sat in one of our salon chairs.

Apparently, our efforts to educate were paying off. Hundreds of other women were beginning to see the true value of what we were offering, and we were getting booked back to back with customers from all over the world. We had never been that busy, even at our peak in the original salon on Bond Street. In fact, our growth was outpacing our capacity to the point where women were wandering all over the house. One customer who arrived early for her appointment went looking for a bathroom and walked into my living quarters downstairs! We were on a roll, eating off our new hair platform—curls. Our phone was blowing up with calls.

REINVENTION

★

We'd taken a calculated risk by completely reinventing our business model, with radically different rules and pricing, based on knowing our worth and taking ownership of our unique aesthetic and skill sets. What we were doing in the Bed-Stuy salon was unheard of for the hair business in our culture. This was like nothing out of the movies *Beauty Shop* or *Steel Magnolias*. Our salon was not a location for neighborhood women and friends to hang around and gossip. It wasn't a loud, messy, chaotic environment. We ran our business with an almost Zenlike quiet and efficiency. A distracting salon environment would not have worked for me. I need

The Pros of Natural Hair

★ You can get back to your God-given natural hair texture, which is thicker, denser, and much stronger than relaxed and processed hair.

★ Exploring natural hair can be an enlightening and positive process of self-discovery.

★ There is freedom from styling hair if you plan on wearing it free-form.

★ The natural-hair community is a fascinating social space. You'll make new friends who are sharing your journey, and be part of a conversation.

★ You may feel a greater sense of pride, self-love, and self-acceptance.

★ No more harsh chemicals that can damage hair follicles and scalp.

★ Less time in weekly or monthly salon visits.

★ It is a chance to rock cool new styles such as straight, Afro-braided, curled, and rolled.

★ Natural hair often has many textures, like an intricate piece of art.

★ Many regal hairstyles have been achieved with curls, kinks, and waves.

★ History has showcased highly textured hair over the years, from kings and queens, like Louis XIV and Queen Elizabeth I, to Marie Antoinette and even Albert Einstein!

a serene atmosphere to bring out my best. I took inspiration from my first salon employer, Joseph, and established strict rules to protect the ambience and enhance efficiency. The calm would relax our clients and better prepare them for a radical improvement in their hair.

Inspired by that little nail salon in downtown Brooklyn, before a time slot was booked and a customer even stepped onto our parlor floor, a credit card deposit was made over the phone. This deposit was applicable to the overall cost of the service should the client decide to proceed with styling, which she typically did. The purpose of taking a deposit was three-fold: It discouraged people from canceling at the last minute; it covered the salon's time if an information-thirsty person just wanted to absorb knowledge without investment; and it en-sured that a record of the client was on file. As isolated as we were, and with my son upstairs, we couldn't be too careful. We also had to make sure our customers were fully committed to making the journey out to Bed-Stuy. Second thoughts could have been costly to our enterprise.

When the clients arrived, we would greet them and ask them to fill out our questionnaire listing their hair history, goals, lifestyle, and frustrations. It was similar to a doctor's form, let-ting us know the last time they received a chemical treatment, the condition of their hair, what they liked and didn't like about their look. It was a holistic approach that allowed me to get to know individuals quickly and better meet their expectations.

Plan for change. Change can be scary, but a well-thought-out transition should lessen fears.

Of course, we would talk to them as well. There's nothing like speaking face-to-face to pick up on who they are and how they would like to see themselves. People came to us for many reasons, whether to make a drastic change, like the Big Chop—cutting off all that dry and chemically damaged hair to make a fresh start—or just to tweak and refine a look they were mostly happy with. Sometimes we had to work to get it out of them, because a lot of women didn't know how to express what they wanted—usually because they didn't know that it was possible. Once we understood what they desired, I had to physically examine the hair, determine its condition and feel its texture for myself, to make sure the goals were realistic. This helped me to see what the possibilities were.

TEXTURE TYPING

★

Around this time, people in online chatrooms had begun typing hair textures using a number and letter system. Andre Walker, Oprah's stylist, wrote a book on this topic, establishing broad hair catergorization to help women understand his advice on hair. The naturally-curly movement took it a step further and got more detailed.

Although Titi and I considered adopting the texture typing system, it was hard to make it stick. Clients were coming to us for information and direction on their hair with no clue about how their natural hair behaved after being relaxed for so many years. We found the exchange much more productive and helpful when we used words instead of numbers to describe the characteristics of their hair. This more descriptive approach was beneficial for us as well as our clients, because it enabled us to identify all of the nuances of the hair before we gave advice or administered any service.

Using words to describe one's hair also helped clients get to know their hair. We helped them articulate all of the things that made their hair what it was. We used words like "curly," "kinky," or "wavy" as benchmarks and elaborated from there, using other descriptions like "thick," "fine," "shrinkage," "straight," "coarse," "dense," "multi-textured," "heat- or color-damaged." We drilled down and got to the bottom of our clients' hair story. We called this exercise the "Hair Narrative."

I loved being part of the process of helping someone to find her best self physically. Playing a role in helping a woman find personal fulfillment, however small that role was, was deeply gratifying. I enjoyed the fellowship with these women. It required a relationship built on trust. I was always candid with our clients, often to the point of telling them something they did not want to hear. When a client called or walked in, Titi and I never lied and said I could deliver something that wasn't possible. If her hair was tightly coiled and dense, for example, and she wanted to walk out of our salon looking like she had Beyoncé's weave but all-natural, we would give her a gentle reality check. We would even turn women away if I couldn't deliver on some of their goals. More often, I'd say something like "Okay, I understand this is what you want, but this is what I can do if you are open to it."

Manage expectations

Industries that revolve around beauty and self-esteem can be a minefield of misguided customers who have been fed images that push them to be something they are not.

1. Take the time to consult with the client before starting on the work, to understand her vision and let her know what can realistically be delivered.
2. Convince her to be her best self. She may look at a picture of Halle Berry and think that should be the aspiration, but it's your job to convince her to enhance her own best assets, which were usually right there on her head.
3. Help her to understand that not everything is for everybody. We are all unique, and so is our hair.
4. When you give your customers possibilities that are connected to their own hair type, and not someone else's, they often walk away loving their texture more than the look they thought they wanted.

SETTING THE TONE

★

My work as a stylist was intense, and we needed to be efficient to handle the large volume of traffic. We also wanted to be fair to our customer and give her the best salon experience possible. That was why we decided to take the chaos out of the situation. When someone had an appointment, she couldn't bring a bunch of friends to hang out, make noise, and disturb the other ladies who just wanted to get real solutions for their hair. We wanted to offer them an altogether different solution than they may have been accustomed to. We knew we were going to transform and to deliver our popular kinks-to-curls service, but we wanted the experience to be positive and delightful. Conversation was welcomed, but at the volume you might hear in a teahouse, not a bar. We treated everyone with the utmost courtesy and expected similar consideration from our clientele. They had to be on time to avoid a backlog that would force other customers to wait unnecessarily.

As business picked up, we needed to run the place with assembly-line efficiency, knocking down the time to treat and style curly and often kinky hair from eight hours to three, and enabling me to service as many as twenty-five to thirty clients on a busy day.

It was an enormous amount of work in a short span of time. The process required blowing out the hair before we even took a pair of scissors to it, so we could see exactly what was going on. Then we did an angle and balance cut to create the right shape for curly textures before styling.

We kept things moving using an innovation we called "butterfly assembly line." The salon staff would take turns with each customer to keep things moving down the line. Naturally and highly textured hair is typically more time-consuming, so having one stylist work on a single client from start to finish would be neither productive nor cost-efficient. We landed on each head like a butterfly touches a flower, getting each stage of the process done more quickly. The alternative would have been to assign a single stylist to each customer, which would have pushed our overhead to the point where it would have been unsustainable for the business.

GUERRILLA MARKETING

★

As much as some of our new customers fussed about the location at first, the approach was paying off. By 2003, we'd gained a reputation as the place to go for expert and efficient service.

We had to get the word out more. The *Time Out* article had helped bring in clients from all over the tristate area and we knew there were many more affluent women we could reach locally. In early 2001 I launched a guerrilla marketing campaign, replicated from the time when I was drumming up business for Branch Cleaning Agency. Using a similar template, I designed a flier with detailed descriptions of our trailblazing services, some funky fonts, and playful graphics reminiscent of seventies album covers, an illustration of a girl with big round curls. On the front, it was headlined "Curve Salon: For Girls with Curls." It had our address and an "As Seen in *Time Out New York*" stamp.

I wanted many different types of customers to find something they could relate to, and to get excited about the new kinds of services we were offering. We listed problems in a typeface that suggested customer handwriting, and in big bold text, we offered the solution:

"I hate wearing my curly hair out. It's always in a ponytail. What can I do?"

"The right CUT is critical. Many stylists tend to be intimidated by curly, kinky, or wavy hair. As a result, thinning, notching, and blunt cutting are often methods used to deal with the bulk and texture. At Curve we address the curl pattern and bulk through face framing angles, soft layering, and light slicing. Although heavy thinning, carving, and slicing are methods many stylists use to address curly hair, the client is often left with a cut that is hard to read when trying to style at home. We at Curve not only want you to look good in our salon, but also to be able to handle and maintain your tresses on your own with ease. Our technique allows for a graceful 'growing out' stage. In addition, you will have the versatility of wearing your hair both curly AND straight, because the cut is structured."

That detailed, informational approach was all over the flier, which offered full disclosure about all of our methods, including preparation, deep treatments, and styling methods. We turned our brochure into a mini–hair Bible, taking potential clients through it step by step and talking about the importance of services like wash and blowouts and deep-conditioning treatments:

"Curly, kinky, or wavy hair is inherently dry and porous. Because of the dryness, oils, waxes, and silicones are piled on to add moisture and control the curl. The buildup from these products can prevent hair from breathing and may cause further damage, frizz, and dehydration. Our deep conditioner penetrates each strand with a two-way moisturizing system that attracts moisture to parched areas as it seals in lubricants. The hair is pliable and softer. At Curve we apply our deep treatment to cover your entire mane. You are then placed under a warm setting for twenty minutes. The heat allows the treatment to penetrate the hair shaft. Your thirsty hair has now been quenched."

For every hair issue, we provided not only a solution but also an approach that was different from what was being offered elsewhere. This enabled our customer to walk out with something that wouldn't require such regular salon visits and that she could maintain at home. The best client was an informed client who understood the purpose behind our process.

This was especially important for our Silkener treatment, which became one of our most sought-after services and continues to be to this day. This chemical process is much less damaging to hair than a full-on relaxer or hair straightener, and it isn't about changing a woman's natural curl by straightening it out of existence. Instead, it serves as a permanent "defrizzant," loosening any kink, curl, or wave, giving it more length, adding uniformity for a silkier, shinier curl pattern. We were moving away from relaxers and straighteners, and this was the compromise. The Silkener uses a mild lye-based chemical of sodium hydroxide (a common ingredient for relaxers), so it doesn't dry out the hair like "no lye" relaxers, especially when we use it in combination with a deep conditioner. The result is more manageable hair that can have the best of both worlds, allowing our customers to wear their hair both curly and straight without the usual frizz and shrinkage. The beauty of the treatment is that it can be easily maintained, doesn't require that awkward period of transition, and requires only a couple of processes a year to keep up.

We laid it all out, trying to catch the attention of women who never knew they had other options for their hair. We wanted to let our customers know we understood their concern and that there was a place for them to go. In addition to describing some of our services, the brochure also described who Titi and I were, the fact that we were of Asian and African-American descent, and that we had experience with all types of naturally curly hair.

I ordered hundreds of the fliers from a printer on Utica Avenue who gave me a good rate. I distributed them all over the higher-income neighborhoods in Brooklyn and Manhattan. We wanted to attract discerning customers who were willing to pay for top-notch service. I covered a lot of ground as I sought out the best neighborhoods, hitting boutiques, cafés, espresso bars, and bistros. We had to get up, get out, and go door-to-door. It was the kind of thing I had done when I was promoting our family cleaning business in Manhattan, though a much more upscale version of that "to the streets" marketing tactic. Within days of all our legwork, our phone was ringing nonstop.

REPEAT CUSTOMER

★

One of those callers was Simone Harris, who'd seen my handiwork at a coffee shop on DeKalb Avenue in Clinton Hill. "Hi there, I saw your flier and was wondering when I could come in and see you," she told Titi, who was answering the phones that morning.

"What are you looking to have done?" Titi asked her.

"A rescue!" she said, laughing. "I'm growing out my natural hair, and I have no idea what to do with it!"

Simone was completely unfazed by our location; she lived nearby, in Clinton Hill. When she walked in for her appointment, we liked her immediately. She was young, long-limbed, and lovely, like a gazelle, with big doe eyes and a wide smile. At the encouragement of a boyfriend, she'd done the Big Chop a few months earlier, to get rid of chemically fried and relaxed hair, and now that it was growing, she needed some serious styling.

"I want to have a curly bob of some kind, but I'm afraid of looking like Marge Simpson's sister Selma," she joked, referring to the tight triangular look that could happen if the curl wasn't cut or handled correctly.

The good news was that Simone had a healthy head of hair. It was a thick, tight coil, but not the tightest, and I didn't need to do any damage control. In addition to taking a break from harsh chemical treatments, she was obviously savvy about which products worked best. Like most women with highly textured hair, Simone had a bathroom cabinet full of products she'd tried over the years—what she called her "product graveyard"—and was meticulous about keeping it moisturized and conditioned, always searching for the next great product for her hair type.

Even just a few years before, the popular perception was that natural hair was too distracting for a corporate setting. Although she was a couple of years younger than we were, Simone had a successful career in an advertising firm that featured a multicultural setting more accepting of different ethnic looks.

In short, she was the perfect canvas for me to work on. First, we washed, conditioned, combed out, and blow-dried her hair straight, so that I could see what was really going on with her texture. A lot of stylists like to cut hair wet, but that tends to create even more of a curl pattern and makes it impossible to check the accuracy of your work, leaving the customer to discover those mistakes when she gets home and tries to style it herself.

Once I'd smoothed out Simone's hair with the blow dryer, I carefully cut about an inch all over to clean up the ends. As I went to work, Simone shared a little of her story. We never force clients to engage in conversation at the salon. We sense their mood, and if they want to chat, they can, but if they just want to zone out and relax, that's cool, too. In the three hours she was with us, Simone did both, sharing and joking about the challenges of dating in the city, and the trials and tribulations of balancing good grooming with an active lifestyle. A big reason why she'd done the Big Chop was to free herself from having to always worry about getting her hair wet. She wanted to be able to run, swim, and generally do her thing outside in the wind, rain, or shine. She wanted the freedom that overprocessed hair, weaves, and wigs don't give. That was exactly how I felt when I was cutting off my own relaxed hair.

The cut took some time. I gave her a little layering in the back but was careful not to overdo it. Simone had a lot of variation to her curl: It was loose in the front, tight in the middle, and wavy underneath. That meant the wrong layering would leave it too high at the top, when the goal was to have all that curl cascade down in a loose ringlet. Once the cut was done, I flat-ironed and flipped her hair, like Mary J. Blige's. When she saw the final result in the mirror, her face lit up. "This is as long as it was before it went natural!" Simone told me. "I can't wait for my man to see it!"

I was glad she went away happy. A couple of months later, Simone came back for more. Her hair was growing out faster, and now that she had something close to her desired length, she wanted a look that would be even easier for her to maintain.

"Our easiest style solution to give you wash-and-go curls would be a Silkener to make it longer, looser, more defined, and

Customer Education Checklist

1. Be as transparent as possible. Provide all the information BEFORE you start the process or service.
2. Take the time to patiently explain what is going to happen, why, and the results that can be expected. This is especially important when you are offering something new in the marketplace and there are no other points of reference.
3. Develop a vocabulary to be as descriptive as possible.
4. Remember, a well-informed customer is more likely to walk out a satisfied customer and become repeat business as she works with you to attain her long-term goals. She will value your services more and appreciate that you are involving and treating her as a collaborator in the process.

manageable," I told her. "But we will need to use a chemical to make it happen. Want to try that?"

"What's in it? What does it do?"

I explained the whole process to Simone. It was a touchy subject for some women, and I wanted to be sure she understood each step. Back then, there tended to be two extremes of women: those who relied on straighteners, weaves, and wigs—basically anything to cover up the hair they were born with—and those who were strictly natural. We were encountering more and more of these natural-hair diehards since our reputation as curly specialists had spread, and some were easily offended by the suggestion that we use any kind of chemical treatment. But the Silkener was a nice compromise, and when she understood exactly how it worked, Simone was all for it.

When we were done, she had loose, stretched-out, shiny, and defined curls. "Oh my God, Miko. You know I keep a picture of Pam Grier on my fridge door, to remind me of why I did the Big Chop in the first place. This is how I always wanted my hair to look. It's perfect!"

In between Simone's visits, I started to notice an explosion of business. We had so many bookings, we could barely keep up. In particular, we were noticing a lot of African-American women with naturally curly, untreated hair, often in a really tight kink or coil—exactly the kind of customer I felt was underserved in the market. About a year before we started specializing in curls, whenever we asked these women how they'd heard of us, they mentioned this chat room CurlTalk, on the website NaturallyCurly.com, founded by a woman based in Texas, Michelle Breyer, and her partner, Gretchen Heber. Well before the advent of social media like Facebook, Twitter, and

Foursquare, there was a handful of online chat rooms dedicated to the beginnings of the natural-hair movement as we know it today, often specializing in hair for women of African descent. NaturallyCurly was quickly becoming one of the friendlier hubs and one of the leaders of an underground culture that we were only dimly aware of at the time.

BIRTH OF A MOVEMENT

★

The fact that our curly-hair focus at Curve salon took place around the same time as the birth of this natural-hair discussion was a fortunate coincidence. We were not deliberately dovetailing with this preexisting trend, which had its own origins and momentum. These were women who did not chemically treat their hair as a matter of principle. It was a long overdue backlash against the social norms of striving for bone-straight hair. We were always aware that it was out there, and we understood why it existed, but we'd never consciously connected the dots.

Back then, generally, natural hair as it related to people of African-American, Caribbean, and African descent meant braids, dreadlocks (or locs), barber cuts, and Afros. There were some wonderful locticians, or dreadlock specialists, and natural hair-care providers like legendary Adémola Mandella of Kinapps in Brooklyn and the Locks N' Chops salon. Many businesses were inspired by Adémola, and we started seeing wonderful shops pop up in Brooklyn, like Loose Ends by Kimberly Hendrix and Black Roots by James McDowell on Flatbush Avenue. These salons and stylists did amazing and meticulous work with braids, locs, and extensions. Some of them had a solid barber's background, too. But none of these salons catered to curly hair; natural hair was not even widely referred to as curly at the time. As we drove up Fulton Street, I told my sister, "One day we will see signs hanging outside these salons saying, 'We do curly hair.'"

In the early 2000s, not one salon in this country was using our techniques for curly, kinky, and wavy hair, like shingling—a styling method created by Titi. There were two popular salons in New York City that catered to curly hair: Ouidad and Devachan. Though both companies were innovative and creative, it seemed like their core business was not the tighter-coiled curl that often belonged to women with an African heritage. This represented a phenomenal business opportunity, and who better to do it than us—we had the skills and the hair to go with it!

Until we came along, if your hair was not identifiably naturally curly without the manipulation of a twist or spiral set, curly hair for women of color usually meant a Jheri curl; not many salons or stylists were focusing on this chemical curl service anymore simply because it was out of style. My own experience as a busy mother, and the lack of services for women like me, helped me to realize there was a space for us to make a difference with more specialized services.

Initially, I intended to do only curly hair. The business plan was never race- or ethnicity-specific. Just curls. But after a while I found myself homing in on those with a tighter-coiled curl. I thought these women needed to know they had a treasure right on top of their head. All these years, many thought and were told they had bad hair. But really, it was the best hair in the world, versatile and beautiful. Not only was there potential for a growing business, but also the fact that this customer was not being addressed at all lit a fire in me. I had uncovered one of the biggest misconceptions that generations of women of color had not widely known—black women have naturally curly hair! They did not realize that kinky hair is just tightly coiled curls. The curl was already in there, waiting to be revealed. Many of us did not know it, including Titi and me growing up.

It was surreal to think that we had uncovered something so amazing and had all the styling techniques to handle and showcase it from soup to nuts. This discovery made women come to Bed-Stuy from all over the world to see what we could do for them.

The focus on tighter-coiled hair wasn't to the exclusion of other customers—our business has always been multicultural— but I loved seeing women with textures regarded as "too chal- lenging" for other stylists and being able to show them how their hair could be transformed to its beautiful potential. Their reactions when I held up that mirror and revealed the results never got old. Some were so happy, they cried. It was as if they were seeing their own true beauty for the first time in their lives. We loved being a part of these moments of discovery.

YES TO THE 'FRO

★

This woman was being totally ignored on most fronts, and she deserved better. She had no services, expertise, or products ca- tering to her unique needs. There weren't even any images in the media of the tighter-coiled/kinkier curl. The images that spoke to this highly textured customer were mostly of straighteners and weaves. It was a Eurocentric ideal of beauty—everything she was not, making it hard for this potential client to imagine embracing her God-given hair texture. It was difficult for this customer to imagine how she would be received by friends, family, or the workplace. There were no images to support the fact that highly textured hair is beautiful and can be accepted in the mainstream. There was certainly no information on how to care for it.

If anything, this customer was being insulted by biases and images in the media on a daily basis. In 2007—not so long ago—an editor at *Glamour* notoriously announced to the world, "Just say no to the 'fro," in response to what was seen as professional in the workplace, making millions of women feel bad about what they were born with. Around the same time, radio personality Don Imus infamously called young women "nappy-headed."

But it was what women weren't seeing that had the most impact. At the time, few celebrities would be seen in public without a long pin-straight weave of some sort. There were exceptions, like actress Joia Lee, who was ahead of her time. She had it right as she rocked her natural-textured amber-colored hair with what looked like a loose two-strand twist-out. Actress and comedian Phyllis Yvonne Stickney also wore her natural hair texture in free form. But these women were on the cutting edge.

> *Identify the underserved customer and get to know her needs and desires. It will help you corner the market with a steady stream of loyal clientele.*

Even our clients' own mothers and grandmothers had unintentionally made them feel ashamed of their natural hair, drumming into them the notion that they needed to spend hours under the hot iron, pull their hair back tight, chemically relax it, or hide it under a wig or a scarf. In homes across the country, girls were given the "Ace comb test." If you could pass a lock of hair straight through a fine-tooth comb, it was seen as a sign of beauty. That had to change.

Every culture has its baggage. The view we have of our hair may go back to the days of slavery, when the lighter-skinned women with the straighter hair got to work inside as housemaids. The whiter the look, the greater the preferential treatment, and that thinking may have carried over to the self-hatred tied to hair in its natural state for some.

Even after the Afro culture of the seventies and an Afrocentric boom in the nineties, it's been only in the past couple of years that we've seen beautiful women like Viola Davis, Alicia Keys, and Jill Scott in all their naturally curly glory, as well as the Miss Jessie's customer. People are really embracing big, highly textured, in-your-face curls, and it's gratifying to see how the world is changing. These days you can't turn on the television or look in a magazine without seeing at least one curly girl advertising a product. That relatively new phenomenon has gone mainstream quickly. It is now preferred.

Getting our customers to believe in new possibilities for their hair didn't happen overnight. It required me to be a cross between a self-esteem coach and a curly-hair evangelist. Our customer needed to be told about the naturally gorgeous hair she'd been blessed with, which may have been hidden for many years under relaxers, braids, or weaves. She needed proof that she really did have a valuable and gorgeous texture on her head. After all, natural hair is the only thing that defies gravity. It points straight up to heaven. That has to mean something!

Many of the women we saw did not know what they had, due to straight styling from an early age. These women needed to understand, believe, and trust that they had curls and not unmanageable "kinks and naps." They needed to be reassured that they had good hair and not bad—contrary to what some may have told them over the years or what they may have come to feel about their own hair.

Like any new movement, it required an education. Transitioning to curly hair or back to natural was a matter of teaching our customer how to work with what she had. She needed to understand that hair is a fiber, like cotton or silk, and it can be manipulated with the right techniques and products. Titi and I were studying hair on a granular level, understanding curl

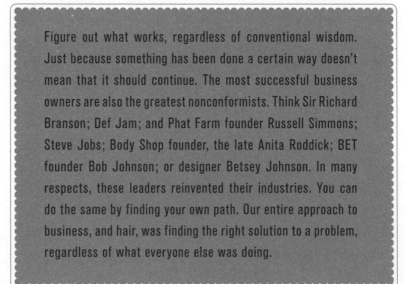

Figure out what works, regardless of conventional wisdom. Just because something has been done a certain way doesn't mean that it should continue. The most successful business owners are also the greatest nonconformists. Think Sir Richard Branson; Def Jam; and Phat Farm founder Russell Simmons; Steve Jobs; Body Shop founder, the late Anita Roddick; BET founder Bob Johnson; or designer Betsey Johnson. In many respects, these leaders reinvented their industries. You can do the same by finding your own path. Our entire approach to business, and hair, was finding the right solution to a problem, regardless of what everyone else was doing.

patterns as individual as thumbprints, and transferring that knowledge to our customer.

Once the client was made aware that the texture she was born with had its own beauty and abilities, she needed change agents like us to help her manifest the look and style she most desired. She honestly did not know what to ask for. She needed to see our positive images and reinforcement through before-and-after pictures to prove that this was real. She needed products to support her brave transition, and finally, she needed courage to make this move. She had choices to make: Big Chop (cutting out all the chemically treated or heat-damaged hair); Transition (easing the gradual growing out process of relaxed hair); Shingling (a special layering effect to better enhance the curl); Two-Strand Twist (a way of defining curls by hand-twisting two sections of hair); or wash-n-go (essentially applying product to damp hair and allowing the natural curl to come forward once dry). All these new decisions could be confusing, even agonizing, but they were also exciting.

CHAT-ROOM BUZZ

★

Much of that enthusiasm was being generated by our new friend Simone in 2001. Unbeknownst to us, Simone was a regular on the NaturallyCurly.com CurlTalk boards and had been posting about our salon. She possessed a whole Shutterfly folder of her hair looks and had been showing the women what we'd done for her, with rave reviews and commentary along the lines of "Hey, guys, I got my hair blown out for the first time today since going natural. I went to a place called CURVE salon for a trim. Ladies, if you are in Brooklyn, CHECK THIS PLACE OUT!"

She continued to post, showing how her hair was growing out, sharing how she was styling and maintaining at home, and telling everyone about each visit to Curve, constantly posting pictures of her tresses before and after. The women were fascinated, but when she raved about the Silkener process and described how it gave her a more uniform curl, she got some serious backlash from some of the more militant natural-hair members. In one hilarious posting Simone described being "kicked off of nappy island."

"Traitor!" one of the posters wrote. "You're not natural anymore!" said another. "That stuff is creamy crack!" "You have been lying all along and using chemicals in your hair," the gang continued. "That's not your real texture!"

Simone defended herself. She desired the kind of curly hair that would allow her to live her life and not have to think twice about jumping in the water at Martha's Vineyard, or running through the rain if she happened to forget her umbrella. Like the majority of our clients, and naturally-curly women in general, she just wanted her hair to look good, with the ease of maintenance that would free her to live life to its fullest. "We do all kinds of things to beautify. We put on deodorant and lotion. We don't just get up and go. Whether it's hair or makeup, we do things to look a certain way. I just want a nice curl . . ."

The discussions got nasty. This was a lightning-rod topic, and the CurlTalk posters were often in fights about whether you cut your hair dry or wet, whether certain ingredients are kosher if they aren't strictly natural, whether or not it's okay to use silicone. There was a great deal of contention because the topic often touched on a lifetime of self-esteem issues that revolved around skin tone and race. We were sure Michelle Breyer and Gretchen Heber were marveling at how out of hand these spirited women got. Michelle once shared that they had to step in when the topics got too racist, mean, and nasty.

On some level, I got it. Titi and I have never been about political statements when it came to hair. Good grooming is good grooming. But for many, there's a long history of pain associated with natural texture. As many women do, we sometimes define ourselves by the way we look, and hair is one of the first things we see. That's why the discussion was often about much more than hair. At the end of the day, do what you like with your hair. It is absolutely wrong for someone to judge, criticize, and exclude you because of your hair choices.

GOING VIRAL

★

The lesson of all this attention we were getting through Simone, even the attacks, was that we didn't need to spend a dime on advertising. Why would we, when people were already talking about us? There is no more powerful advertising than the recommendation of a satisfied customer.

The chat-room buzz more than made up for the fact that we didn't have a shingle outside our brownstone. It was exactly like that line in the Fabergé Organics shampoo commercial from my childhood: "You'll tell two friends, and they'll tell two friends, and so on, and so on, and so on . . ." But it only took one person talking about us in that space for word of our salon's services to spread like wildfire. Simone had lit the match, and there was no going back.

We chose not to participate directly in the dialogue. It seemed too self-serving to promote ourselves directly to these potential customers, and we wanted to remain above the fray. But in 2002, we built our first website with the help of Simone, who, in addition to being a hair trendsetter, was a tech-savvy young lady with some serious design skills.

Once it was set up, it occurred to me that I wanted to show before-and-after photos. Simone didn't see the need, but she shrugged and gave me a template so that I could upload as many pictures as I wanted. Visuals were key. We were serious about curls, kinks, and waves, and were about to change standard images of beauty by offering a new solution—mostly transitioning kinks to curls. We'd watch the back-and-forth between these women, complaining about a particular hair challenge, and post before-and-after pictures that specifically addressed those concerns. It was a pivotal move.

We didn't even have to say anything. The visuals were powerful enough. And each time we added a picture, it sparked endless dialogue online. We weren't participating in the conversation, but we were stimulating it. Every week we'd upload dozens of pictures, and whenever someone had something negative to say about us, we'd have the hard evidence of our results to prove them wrong. The phone wouldn't stop ringing. We'd gone viral

Feel the pulse. Be close enough to your customer to know exactly what she's thinking, what she needs to hear, and how she's evolving.

before the marketing professionals had even invented the term!

One of the most talked-about issues on the boards was our pricing. Somehow the word "natural" connoted low prices to these women. They didn't realize that treating and styling natural hair is four times the labor. Although it was a labor of love, we just needed to be compensated accordingly, to continue to feel good and not resent our new specialty. It made a few of our customers angry, although it never seemed to deter them from seeking out our services. On our end, there was no denying the work involved, but you would have thought from some of their reactions that we were trying to fleece them. Others were just happy to learn about effective ways to manage and style their hair. We watched these faithful Curve customers' hair grow out curlier and curlier. It was gratifying: exactly the confirmation we needed to stay the course and not mind the naysayers.

THE SPEAKEASY

★

The majority of our clients were an incredible and diverse group of women, many of whom have become lifelong friends. Women in advertising, media, the arts, even finance were coming to us. Our early customers were mostly educated professional types who were looking for something they couldn't get anywhere else—a chance to become better versions of themselves, with healthy, well-groomed hair. One of those women was Emma Robinson, a radio and communications executive at Public Radio Corporations.

Emma had been searching for the right salon for a couple

of years before she came to us. She'd been looking for a curly or wash-and-go look and had tried out a texturizer at another very popular salon that catered to upscale black hair care in New York City. It was the first time she'd had any kind of major chemical treatment since she was sixteen, and she rocked that look for a while, but it didn't feel exactly right to her. When she saw an article about us in *Essence* magazine, she decided to give us a try.

By the time Emma got to my chair, she was growing out the texturizer, and all I could see was damage. It was shoulder-length but not in good condition.

"Hey, you know, if you want a good, uniform curl, we're going to have to cut," I advised her.

Understandably, Emma was resistant to the idea. It can be a heartbreaking decision, because as women, we tend to associate the length of our hair with our femininity. I empathized, because my own transition from relaxed to naturally curly had been rough. I was so intent on avoiding the Big Chop that I had clung to a ratty, curly weave for far too long. Cutting off all that hair can be like losing a limb, and the thought of such a dramatic change sends many of my clients into a panic.

"I want to keep the length," she insisted. "This is my look."

"Okay, but I just want to warn you, the results will be mixed—curly with straight ends," I told her. "It's important that you get back your healthy hair first."

Emma allowed me to trim a little, but she wasn't completely satisfied, and I could sense her frustration. That was why I wanted to make it clear to her what needed to be done and what she could expect if we did less. When my clients don't take my advice, I can't do my best work, but they're not always ready. It's a process, and it takes patience as well as a long-term vision to reach a hair goal.

When your hair doesn't feel right, *you* don't feel right. Emma had always wanted that soft but natural curl. She was a woman who'd been completely natural since she was a teenager. She'd done the braids and cornrows. She'd even done thread wraps, where you wrap silk thread or cotton around your locks. It was an earthy African look and a way to wear her hair as a kind of political statement. Emma comes from that artistic and intellectual world, running African-American programming for radio, and her hair matched her lifestyle and social views. Her hair was expressing her creativity, but as she told me years later, "at some point I crossed over into the belief that hair is just an accessory, and that who you are politically and socially is not necessarily measured by clothes or hair but the person you are."

Emma felt secure enough in herself to know that nothing she did externally would change who she was. Hair became something she could have fun with, a way to look and feel great beyond any statement. She'd moved beyond the angst of those ladies in the chat rooms, because she had the maturity and wisdom to know that being a polished and styled professional woman didn't take away from what she stood for. That's why she came back, ready, willing, and able to do the Big Chop. Luckily, she had a considerable amount of new growth. As a result, she was thrilled with the final cut. She looked fresh and pretty—her curls popped!

I was pleased when Emma came back. She was cautious and analytical, like me: a fellow traveler. Over the years, she became part of a group of interesting women who would sit around our brownstone parlor while waiting for our services, enjoying the snacks and drinks we laid out, listening to jazz, gospel, soul, R&B, or whatever we were playing on the stereo, and talking about life in general. Our Bed-Stuy parlor had transformed into an old-school *salon*—not the hair kind but similar to the places they had back in the day in Paris, those society ladies' homes where artists and thinkers would get together and have serious conversations. Another client—inspired, I guess, by our restored-brownstone decor—compared us to a Prohibition-era speakeasy, a happening place that you had to be in the know in order to find.

There was something thrilling about seeing the caliber of women embracing what Titi and I were doing. There was a cool factor to the environment we'd created, and these were the insiders who got us.

"I love the underground feel of this place," Emma once told me. "It feels like we are part of something significant."

"What do you mean?" I asked her.

"I mean, innovations in African-American women's hair have been few and far between. This is the third time someone has created a leap in manipulating hair, from straight, to Afro, and now this natural curl. By giving women the tools to do this, you have spearheaded the next big wave in our culture."

Emma was right. Over a couple of years, we had become a destination, and women were coming to us from as far away as England, Africa, the Caribbean, and Brazil, as word spread about the solutions we were offering and the undeniable results. As Titi and I looked around at the hundreds of women we served each month, we began to realize that this movement was by no means confined to one ethnicity. Curve's impact went far beyond the specialized market we'd originally envi-

sioned. Black, Hispanic, Middle Eastern, Jewish, Caucasian—
women of all races and nationalities were part of a core group
of loyal customers, and their curly-textured hair was the fiber
that united them.

A case in point was Michelle Breyer, the founder of Natu-
rallyCurly.com and now a dear friend. A nice Jewish woman
with a head of beautifully coiled hair, Michelle had spent most
of her youth trying to straighten the life out of it.

"I used to live in fear of people knowing how curly my hair
was," Michelle shared with us recently. "Foggy weather would
ruin my day."

Like a lot of us, Michelle grew up at the mercy of her hair,
feeling the pressure to conform to beauty ideals like Christie
Brinkley, Cheryl Tiegs, and Farrah Fawcett. She was constantly
fighting what she was born with, and there were days she didn't
even want to leave the house.

Frustrated that there was
nothing out there for women like
her, like us, Michelle, a journal-
ist, decided to launch Naturally-
Curly in 2000 as a side hustle,

> *Be open to every kind of
> customer. Catering to a
> broader demographic can
> reap unexpected rewards.*

and the website rapidly developed an international following. A
year later, we came along, arming women with information and
tools that could empower them. We didn't simply tell them what
could be done, we showed them.

But the advice didn't come just from us. Our salon became
a kind of lab where our customers could sit with each other to
exchange ideas and related experiences. Women with similar
hair types would find their hair twins and swap tips on products and home maintenance. The volume of women we saw

revealed certain trends and patterns in hair issues, and the looks they were trying to achieve foretold the next wave of hair fashion. They told us what products they bought off the shelf, what worked and what didn't. We listened carefully, learning more in each conversation about our customers' different hair challenges and filing away the feedback for future use.

Titi and I were paying attention to the fact that we needed more reliable products to support this thrust of clients with specific needs. We were mixing and matching existing products on the market, but nothing was quite right. It was a months-long process that took time and effort on top of running the salon. But knowing we were on the right path kept us motivated. We had something in mind, something that would transform the lives of not just our salon customers but curly-haired women worldwide.

Eight

THE BEST DAMN CURL CRÈME, PERIOD!

Go against the rules or ignore the rules.
That is what invention is about.

—HELEN FRANKENTHALER

Hearing the roar of the engine as the truck pulled up to the curb, ready to handle our business, everyone in the house at 120 Hancock Street sprang into action.

"Ti-tiiiii, they're here!" I screamed up to the fourth floor.

"I'm coming down now! Where are my gloves so I can lift those boxes?" Titi shouted. "Come on, find that hand truck so we can start loading. Let's go, let's go!"

We had it down to a science, mobilizing our little army of five helpers to load and unload the truck in half an hour.

Our whole day revolved around getting these orders filled. It was literally a cottage industry in the heart of Brooklyn's urban landscape.

Anyone walking into our brownstone in those days would have been hit with a waft of the most intoxicating scents: vanilla, peppermint, coconut, berries, and tropical fruits. But what they would have seen was quite a contrast from what these lush scents conjured up. The exposed brick walls of our brownstone's cellar had been painted white for extra brightness and set up specifically to handle our daily domestic production, with separate staging areas for each phase. In the back of the room, Titi, our crew, and I stood for hours at a counter, mixing batches of curl magic with a row of four industrial-grade Hobart mixers. Then we moved the tubs of product to a table in the middle, pouring the mixture into a Simplex machine, filling jar after jar with precisely measured amounts.

So that we could sit up close to our work, we used wood and metal school chairs that we'd retrieved from a trash dump, and we cut the legs off long metal industrial tables. This ensured that our process was exact, avoided spillage, and saved our backs from giving out while pouring heavy buckets of cream into the jar fillers.

Once the filling was done, the minimal assembly line moved to a work area in the front, where we had our label machine set up. After all caps were shut tight, we carefully affixed a label to each jar by hand, packaging them up way before orders came in so we wouldn't get overwhelmed if we had a surge in orders on a particular day. Each week, at our peak, we had to get about a thousand jars ready to go.

It was 2005, a little over a year into production of Curly

Pudding, our naturally curly hairstyling product that was our heaviest formulation, aimed at a tighter-coiled texture, and our most popular at the time. We were producing a similar but different formulation called Curly Meringue, a medium-weight hold and the first in our series of "heavier curl" crèmes for Miss Jessie's stylers, which helped hold curls in place longer for wash-and-go curly styles, rod sets, and two-strand twists (see glossary at the back for definitions and a complete list of product descriptions). That year we were also producing Curly Buttercreme, to style, soften, and moisturize dry-textured hair, keeping it healthy. Customers loved its tingling scalp sensation, as well as the natural sheen the product gave to hair.

Invest in what you need. You must have the proper tools when running a business. Shortcuts will lead to more labor and less efficiency, increasing operational costs.

We were manufacturing a lot of product from a basement operation. Within a matter of months since the creation of our first product, our brownstone had turned into a center of operations for manufacturing, distribution, order fulfillment, and shipping.

We didn't outsource any part of the process and had no one but ourselves to deal with the incoming email orders (and we accepted payment via PayPal): When we were starting up our own business, we did whatever it took with whatever resources we had. No one could tell us it couldn't be done, and not knowing any better was exactly why we worked day and night to make our dreams materialize. We did it all, and repeated each process day after day, with barely enough time to come up for air, because those UPS trucks kept on coming. The pickups and deliveries occurred several times a week.

Once they were parked outside, we had to be ready. And quick. The last thing we wanted was an extended scene, so we went to great lengths to avoid attracting too much attention. The less people knew about our business, the better.

ROUGH DIAMOND

★

The folks on our street were harmless, even silently protective of the nice sisters who'd moved in two years earlier. They liked that we were different, appearing to be young women from the other side of the tracks, and that we *chose* to live in this neighborhood. We had always assumed that gave us instant acceptance by a community of people who'd been living on this stately but forgotten block of brownstones for generations. The neighborhood had a few pockets like this—some gems amid the ruins of urban decay—that showed the pride and dignity of the longtime residents, who worked hard to preserve these grand old houses, some of which were even mansions. There was a certain grace about parts of Bedford-Stuyvesant, and that was what had drawn us there. We always knew it was a diamond in the rough with lots of potential.

Bedford-Stuyvesant was once the largest ghetto in North America. Beyond Hancock and a handful of other streets, the blocks were sketchy. We had to put bars on the windows of the first floor because the first year we moved in, someone tried

A Complete Guide
from Concept to Marketplace

1. Once you've found that big idea, set the standard for quality and innovation.

2. Source only the best possible ingredients or components to ensure that you are not just the first to market but the best. This will ensure that when the competition catches on, you will keep your customer's loyalty.

3. Research, research, research! Use circles of your friends, peers, clients, whomever you are targeting, as an informal testing lab. Get honest feedback and use it.

4. Once the concept has been developed and the prototype has been created, start small. If you have to work out of your garage, kitchen, or basement, so be it.

5. When you have your formula or prototype ready, protect your intellectual property! Patent it. Research what type of patent or patents your product needs, and do the paperwork. When you are ready to go to a manufacturer, you will own the formula and be able to take it with you anywhere.

6. As you get ready to launch, use grassroots marketing to get the word out. Let your brand's reputation build by word of mouth.

7. Be witty and informational in your packaging.

8. Leverage social media and start building personal relationships with smaller vendors who will carry your product.

9. Send out press releases and fliers to every media outlet you can think of. A little free PR, such as a glowing write-up in a trade or consumer publication, can take your start-up to the next level.

to break in; our dog, Rheggi Bear, barked his ass off while we slept, scaring away our intruder. As soon as we went downstairs and saw that the doorknob was broken off, we knew what was up, and shifted into high alert.

When we first moved to the area, it was mostly empty lots, tagged and grimy cement walls, burned-out buildings, random auto shops, and corner bodegas. Many of the once-stately brownstones had been turned into rooming houses, stripped of their historic period detail, converted to rent out rooms that would pay the mortgage. In addition to the black folks who'd migrated from the South decades earlier, the area was full of immigrants from the Middle East, the West Indies, and Africa—street vendors selling incense and CDs—as well as Dominicans and Puerto Ricans. Although it was a known area in New York for low-income occupants, Bed-Stuy made up one of the most ethnically diverse populations in the country. The projects, including the Marcy Houses (former home of Jay-Z), were not far from us, on Nostrand Avenue, and questionable characters were always loitering on Bedford Avenue and Fulton Street, so we had to keep our operation on the down-low. Year by year, the neighborhood was improving, but if word had spread that we had a flourishing business going on right in the 'hood, who knew what could have happened.

Be aware of your surroundings and invest in security. Small-business owners have too much to lose.

Early on, we took our last savings to invest in a top-shelf security system with cameras and alarms at every entrance and window, in case of another break-in. It wasn't just that our operation was valuable. We were scared to death because we were alone, with no man present and with a little baby in the house; we had to do all we could to protect ourselves.

LACE CURTAINS

★

There were too many eyeballs on us as it was. On that wet afternoon in April, as we maneuvered the hand truck up the stairs from the basement entrance of our house, careful not to drop any of the packages, our neighbors were already gathering on their stoops or sliding back their curtains to check out what we were doing. We noticed Maurice, who lived next door, standing in his usual spot at his front window on the second floor, with his peppered white hair, wearing a stained white undershirt, shorts, and gray slippers, watching us with curious eyes. Ours was a quiet, leafy street, with a good handful of folks who were unemployed and stayed home all day. It wasn't a stretch to say we'd become their daily entertainment. Certainly, they were intrigued about what was going on, although thankfully, nobody ever asked.

What they saw was the two of us and a couple of people who worked in our hair salon, like busy little ants with our pushcarts, swiftly loading product, which was all boxed and ready for pickup by the UPS man, Jeff, who pulled up on our block every day like clockwork at four P.M.

"Hey, ladies, how you doin' today?" he asked us, jumping out of the driver's seat to scan each item and help us with the boxes. Jeff was always cool about extending himself. "Dag, y'all got a whole lot of boxes! What's in there?"

It was a typical daily order, with packages of the most highly sought-after products in hair care to be sent to our online customers. With no advertising, just reviews from loyal customers on the Internet, we'd attracted a passionate cult following that was quickly spreading to the mainstream as magazines such as *O, Lucky, Allure,* and *Essence* discovered who we were and announced the curl-enhancing qualities of our products to the rest of the world.

The numbers were growing steadily every day. Through our website, women (and a few men) were writing in from all over the country, requesting product. Business was coming in fast, and we could barely keep up. As Miss Jessie would say, we were up to our ears in "high cotton."

In addition to the daily delivery, there was a monthly delivery of fifty-five-gallon drums of liquids and oils for the next batch's run, brought to us on a tractor trailer so huge it could hardly squeeze down our narrow residential street. It wore us out, lifting and rolling those huge barrels into our small home factory, which could barely contain the production materials and equipment. If our neighbors only knew what we were up to in that converted basement of ours, with the assembly lines and constant hum of machinery. Deep inside our brownstone, it was the birth of an industry.

It was almost too scary to acknowledge what was happening in our lives at that juncture. Titi and I were an unlikely pair at an unlikely place and time. Overnight, our salon and product business were exploding, and we were insanely busy. We didn't have the time or inclination to lift our heads up and see where we were or how we'd gotten to that point. All we were doing was getting our grind on, never stopping for a minute to think: *This is it. We did it!*

SOMETHING FROM NOTHING

★

This was just the beginning. Using our imagination and our hands, we not only built a successful business, but we also were about to revolutionize the beauty industry. We created something from nothing.

The rapid growth began with a product we'd created on our kitchen table two years earlier, in 2003—the first leave-in styler for the tighter-coiled texture that defines curls, cuts frizz, and adds shine and moisture. Depending on how much was used, it created a looser, wavier texture. In the past, when people with a tighter-coiled texture wanted a more relaxed curl, they had to constantly feed their hair with wet activators to counteract the harsh double processing required to get that look from a Jheri Curl. Those treatments never dried, creating a Soul Glo greasy look. But we'd finally found a non–chemically altering styling formula that produced curls without harsh heat and chemical processing, leaving hair healthy and conditioned. It was something no other formulation targeting tighter-coiled hair had been able to do. It was truly revolutionary.

We couldn't wait to try out our latest concoction downstairs on our toughest critics: our clients.

"It's so fluffy and creamy, it looks like pudding!" one of our regulars exclaimed.

"Oh my God, it even smells delicious!" chimed in another.

All of a sudden, it occurred to us what we should call it—Curly Pudding. It was perfect, because our approach was exactly what our grandmother used to do in her kitchen all the time, making that irresistible banana pudding. It was all about the color, texture, and consistency. It became the standard we applied to all of our hair products. Not only must it look, smell, and feel good, but it must work well, too.

Beyond the appealing scent and texture, our clients loved how it made their hair look. It wasn't our original intent to make something for retail. It was just something we planned to have on hand in our salon, to better service our clients and deliver on our new curly-service menu more effectively and reliably. But people kept asking us if we had some to sell. They wanted to take home supplies of Curly Pudding to tide them over between salon visits.

We bought a couple of six-quart KitchenAid mixers for making larger batches. The trick was to remember the exact order and amounts of the ingredients, how they were mixed, for how long, which stage of the process required heating or cooling. It wasn't just the ingredients, it was a recipe, and it had to be duplicated exactly, repeating the same quantities and sequences of mixing and blending to keep the product perfectly consistent.

LIKE NO OTHER

★

We also stockpiled containers. If we were going to start making batches of the formula, we figured we might as well put our stamp on it. I called on my friend Garrett for help. I had admired his clean, edgily graphic skills at *New Word Magazine* but couldn't nail them on my own at first. What we didn't want was something that looked like the stereotypical products targeted to customers with tightly coiled hair. Interestingly, the manufacturers of products for this market did not share the same hair issues. We also did not want our product to resemble something one would find in the back of a health food shop or market stall. Instead, we wanted a more prescriptive, apothecary look that evoked something down-home and reliable.

The references to pudding, and the fact that it really was a recipe, gave us the idea to present our product like one. I worked with a local graphic designer to come up with labels that resembled old-fashioned recipe cards, with a doily border and detailed descriptions of the jar's contents. This product would look, smell, and feel like no other in our customer's medicine cabinet. The labels also referenced old circus posters and newspaper ads, with newsprint on doily-motif labels and content that was detailed, informative, prescriptive, and fun. Presenting the information in the right format was key.

First we had to come up with a brand name. For a minute we toyed with the idea of "Curl Labs Incorporated." It separated the product from the salon, which we thought we needed to do, fearing the association with a boutique business in Bed-Stuy wouldn't be high-end enough or taken seriously. But that name was too boring, sterile, and obvious. Then it was "The Best Damn Curl Crème, Period," which our mother did not like at all. "Too boastful," she said. Finally, it was named Miss Jessie's, after our beloved grandmother.

OUR NAMESAKE

—————————————————————— ★ ——————————————————————

The decision to name our product business after our grand-mother and to take inspiration from her recipes occurred around the same time. She'd been on our minds. In 2001, shortly after my son was born, Miss Jessie had passed after complications from a stroke. It was an especially huge loss for me, because we used to talk every single morning and night. She was my rock when we were going through the transition of moving our business to Bed-Stuy, and my constant emotional support as I was dealing with that first year of mother-hood. Titi and I both missed her terribly and wanted to pay tribute to this great woman who'd taught us a lot from an early age.

In 2005, Titi decided we should also named the salon after our grandmother. By then our product had such a huge cult following, there was no way an association with our brownstone salon could hurt us. Quite the opposite. Since our inspiration was coming from the salon, it made sense to have the continuity, with one side of the business reinforcing the other. The name Curve had served us well, but we had a sense that we were moving on to something bigger.

The name also evoked memories of all those times my sister and I sat with Miss Jessie around the kitchen table, whipping up everything from hair pomade to cake batter as she taught us how to create something life-enhancing out of the few resources we had. What could be more fitting? Miss Jessie was the ultimate mother of invention, and we were bor-rowing all her moves.

The name and its personal story just happened to be a stroke of genius marketing, because many of our customers have a strong woman in their life like Miss Jessie whom they respect and look up to. It was not a conscious decision at the time—we were just proud of our story and going on pure instinct.

Back then, there was no product specifically for curly hair that was named after a delicious dessert-like pudding, buttercream, or meringue. Our labeling—which evoked images of someone nurturing and folksy, with a touch of Southern grace—would eventually become the standard for dozens of other brands. Aunts and uncles started to pop up as names of brands in the curly- and natural-hair space. We started to see puddings, buttercremes, milkshakes, smoothies, soufflés, custards, and more food references than you'd find on a restaurant menu or our grandmother's kitchen table! There was even a company that put Miss Jessie's logo and product name on its jar to entice customers.

At first we did not know what to think. It was surreal to watch all of these developments, because we knew the origins of the trend: our beloved grandmother and everything she stood for, which we represented in a jar of curl magic.

SMOOTH OPERATOR

★

Once we had the product and brand names figured out, we had to come up with ad copy for the labels. Since nothing like this existed, the right messaging was key. We wanted to put all the information that would be helpful to our customer right on the jar. We wanted to talk directly to her. It was our own version of informational and educational advertising—the same approach I'd applied years before when I designed the fliers for our curly-hair services, and even when I made that brochure for Branch Cleaning Agency. It had to clearly and completely answer three questions:

How does it work?

Why is this for me?

What makes it different?

The result, on our earliest edition of Curly Pudding, read like this:

Our world-famous Curly Pudding is a "smooth operator" that transforms shrunken kinks to super-shiny stretched-out curls. Instructions for use: Apply a palmful of Curly Pudding to damp, freshly shampooed and conditioned hair. Rake through large sections and air-dry. For maximum

The more information, the better

1. Use your label as an opportunity to clearly communicate value to your customer.
2. Be specific. Not everything is for everybody. Women need to understand which product is for them and why.
3. In addition to attractive packaging, include witty and engaging text that tells the story of your product.

elongation, comb a nickel-sized dollop through small sections and air-dry. Great for: Tight-Curly, Kinky, and Transitioner's hair.

Underneath the name "Curly Pudding" was a tagline, "The Best Darn Curl Crème, Period!" We were just calling it as it was, the way Miss Jessie herself would have said it, although she was more likely to have said, "The best *damn* curl crème, period!"

CULT FOLLOWING

★

We put Curly Pudding on our website, thinking we might be able to sell a few jars. Boy, were we wrong. It caught fire right away.

Those real-life before-and-after photos didn't hurt. We used good-looking but ordinary people to demonstrate the amazing results of our products and unique styling techniques. No chemically altering ingredients were used to achieve the natural styling looks. It was almost unbelievable. Some even thought we were posting before-and-afters of curly-hair weaves.

People loved the fact that our products had already been road-tested and enthusiastically endorsed by salon customers. At this stage of product and business development, it was necessary to have both elements in place: The salon connoted expertise and gave us unique credibility. Even today, it's through our salon services that Miss Jessie's maintains its intimate relationship with our customers and gets a direct line on their needs, which in turn generates more ideas for product development. We are never at a loss for what to come out with next, because we are on the pulse of what's truly needed, and we understand all the nuances and special ingredients a product should have in order to perform.

But there was another intangible contributing to our products' immediate popularity. When we launched Curly Pudding, our salon already had a kind of unattainable aura, which we deliberately cultivated. There is a bar that is something of an institution in Manhattan's East Village called Please Don't Tell, or PDT. It's both hard to access and next to impossible to find unless you are in the know. The place is located by a hot dog stand and a telephone booth that front the camouflaged entrance of a speakeasy. That was us. We had no sign on our door, we didn't advertise, and only a select few knew our address. That gave our salon a kind of clandestine allure.

That word-of-mouth buzz rubbed off onto Curly Pudding. Suddenly, there was this hot new product that friends were telling each other about, made in this high-priced salon in the 'hood by these two girls who were curl experts. Everyone had to have it. But they couldn't get it. Unless you knew about our website—and back in 2004, that wasn't the first place people thought to look—you had to make an appointment to see us for styling purposes. And, as mentioned, when you made the appointment, you had to make a deposit. The fact that we made it

> *Keep some mystery. When a product seems less attainable, it gives customers the sense that they are getting something truly special.*

hard to get, with many layers to pass through just to get in the door, somehow worked to our advantage. Our being unattainable made people crazy for our product.

STAKEOUT

★

Not that things didn't get a little out of hand in the beginning. Many had heard about us from discussion boards, but they didn't know how to secure an appointment unless someone let them in on the secret. A few women didn't have the patience to wait their turn and thought it would be a good idea to track us down in Bed-Stuy and stake out our brownstone. Typically, they would park across the street, car engines idling as they watched for signs of life through our front windows. It didn't matter if we were home or not. For security purposes, we had a strict policy about not letting anyone in the house unless they had an appointment. We'd also noticed that some of these women on the chat boards were downright angry and hateful. We had dozens of random women ringing our doorbell at all hours of the day, night, weekends, even Sundays, and we had no idea what we were in for if we opened the door. With my son inside, and a business operation we were intent on keeping on the down-low, it made me nervous.

If they rang the doorbell during the daytime, unscheduled, we told them nicely through the intercom to make an appointment. People were dumbfounded. A few were insulted. "But I came all the way here!" one woman exclaimed. "Are you telling me my money's not good enough?"

"I'm sorry, it's just the rules," we told her. "But you're always welcome to call us for an appointment."

We weren't about to make exceptions. The last thing we wanted was impromptu visits from people we didn't know. We feared an influx of customers that we could not manage. We didn't want to be slammed on the chat boards. An open-door policy also would have exposed us to too many prying eyes in the neighborhood. Besides the fact that we were private people, we didn't want people from the area coming in who may have been unprepared for our prices and were likely to ask for a friendly neighborhood discount. It wasn't the kind of conversation we wanted to have. And God forbid too many people would find out what we had going on and report us to The Man. This was an entirely underground operation, and we intended to keep it that way.

Soon after, we started receiving large orders from Louis Licari's, a high-end Fifth Avenue salon in Manhattan. That location was the first place where customers could buy our products outside of our brownstone in Brooklyn.

Next, to meet the overwhelming demand, we picked up our first retailer—Sodafine, a hip consignment shop on DeKalb and Vanderbilt in Clinton Hill run by these two cool white girls. They were actually our second intended stop. We first visited another hip thrift shop on Fulton Street, in Fort Greene, operated by a duo who used to feature those magnificent soul album covers in their storefront. Without skipping a beat, they told Titi they were not interested in carrying Miss Jessie's. When we walked into Sodafine, located on the parlor floor of a brownstone, the owners stared blankly at us. We must have said something right in our pitch, because the more we spoke

Mother's Day (Jessie Mae Branch, *far left*).

Natural girl (Miko, age five, *left*); Titi in the mix, Miko looking on (*right*).

Sisters.
(Titi, *left*; Miko, *right*)

Our pool! Enjoying fruits
of the sales from our first
lemonade stand.

We are family (Titi, *left*; Miko, *right*).

Jimmy Branch—Dad—
always sharp.

Bonding in Daddy's car.

Jamaica, Queens, 127th Street (Miko and Titi, *front and center*).

Introspective young Miko (*below*);
I did my own hair!
(Miko, fourth grade, *right*)

PUBLIC SCHOOL
193
QUEENS
1980-81
CLASS 5-202

Only spot in the bunch (Miko, *second row, center*).

CURLy

Early marketing materials for Focus on Curls (circa 2002, *left*). First ad ever to capture Wash-n-Go Curly Styling, the Miss Jessie's Way. (Curly Pudding used, *below*).

Curve Salon photo shoot—early marketers (Titi and Miko). Check out the '90s lip liner!

Family over everything!

OVER 20 YEARS OF HAIRCARE EXPERTISE
FROM THE MAKERS OF MISS JESSIE'S.
www.missjessies.com

Iconic Miss Jessie's ad for Multicultural Curls.

Our first photo shoot in the Brooklyn brownstone for *Women's Wear Daily* article.

Titi getting ready for BET gifting suite.

Our first warehouse (Brooklyn Navy Yard at 43 Hall Street).

My own Big Chop moment!

My 'fro: growing out my "Big Chop" (Miko).

Titi about to transition to curly hair.

Welcome to our 'hood! Nostrand Avenue Station to Curve Salon (Bedford-Stuyvesant, Brooklyn).

Thriving business at the Bedford-Stuyvesant brownstone.

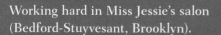
Working hard in Miss Jessie's salon (Bedford-Stuyvesant, Brooklyn).

Titi is a true beauty.

My mother to the rescue (Karen "Yayoi" Matsumoto holding newborn Faison).

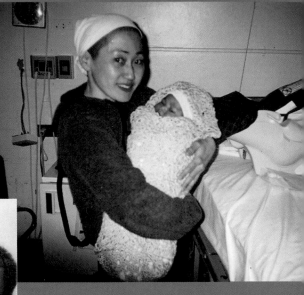

"The Weave" that started it all—our focus on curly hair (Miko with son, Faison).

Natural family (Miko and Faison, Fort Lauderdale, Florida, 2002).

First time seeing Miss Jessie's products in Target; Titi—always the perfectionist—organizing the products (Atlantic Terminal, Brooklyn, New York).

Curly Pudding—our very first product, which revolutionized the hair industry. The best darn curl crème, period.

Innovative cutting technicians: angle and balance cutting method developed by Miko.

Tag team: the Miss Jessie's Butterfly Technique (Titi, *left*, Miko, *right*).

Miss Jessie's moving to SoHo, New York (Titi, *left*, Miko, *right*).

Raw space of Miss Jessie's Studio Salon, SoHo, New York (Titi, *left*, Miko, *right*, 2010).

Miss Jessie's salon store (SoHo, New York).

Miss Jessie's carries on the legacy. SoHo salon opening, 2010
(Miko, *far left*; A'Lelia Bundles, the great-great-granddaughter
of Madam C. J. Walker, *middle*; Titi, *right*).

about our product, the more receptive they became, and soon we were negotiating a deal. We had no idea what we would sell it to them for, but we were so desperate to get the product in a public space and out of our house that we came up with a 60/40 split in their favor. The young female owner, Rebecca, called us back later and said, "Why don't we do it for 50/50?" We were relieved by her suggested split and jumped on it. That original deal was the same one we used with our retail partners for many years.

This transaction meant that when women knocked on our door in Bed-Stuy, we had a place to send them. Sodafine quickly informed us that they couldn't keep enough product on the shelves; before long, our product ended up accounting for a huge portion of their overall sales. In 2004, it was thirty-eight dollars for a professional-salon-sized sixteen-ounce jar. Women traveled for miles to buy Curly Pudding from Sodafine.

With our new local distribution at Sodafine, I wanted to direct new customers who wanted our product to Sodafine so we took out local ads in the *Park Slope Reader* (focusing on the Park Slope section of Brooklyn) and *Our Time Press* (focusing on Bedford-Styuvesant, Crown Heights, Clinton Hill, and Fort Greene). We understood that we needed to chronicle and capture this new hair aesthetic—free-form Afro curly hair. By this time we'd learned how to shoot our own pictures and invested in photography equipment—everything from cameras, fancy lenses, lighting, to backdrop paper—because we did not have the money to pay photographers while building our business back up. We were expert at turning kinks to curls at this point and asked one of our clients, writer/director Dominga Martin, if we could shoot her and her Miss Jessie's curls. She said yes and we knew we produced the first ad in the world showcasing this new hair trend—no one else was doing or even thinking about it at the time.

COVERT OPERATION

★

Many people were clamoring for our product. We ramped up production, moving it from the kitchen table of Titi's fourth-floor apartment in our brownstone, where we were whipping up batches in the KitchenAids, to our garden first floor. Meanwhile, I'd decided to invest in those four industrial-sized Hobart mixers—the kind pizzerias and bakeries use—so that we could mix much larger quantities to meet the increasing volumes of orders. That move increased our output sixfold.

It had become clear that the work was backbreaking for Titi and me. We hired a lovely man we'd met at a hardware store on Atlantic Avenue. He had a work ethic like nothing we'd seen outside of ourselves. I have an instinct for people and was impressed with how this gentleman went out of his way to help load a heavy hand truck into the trunk of our car.

The extra pair of strong hands freed Titi to focus on all the other new challenges of the business, such as shipping, packaging, and not least, sourcing ingredients for our product. Getting all these ingredients shipped to our brownstone was a delicate business. At that point, our typical order might be a thousand boxes of a particular ingredient; obviously, we weren't going to find these quantities in a beauty supply store.

Instead, Titi found a way to contact a product's manufacturer by looking up its name on the label. The manufacturer would in turn hook her up with the distributor. She'd make a direct deal with the distributor, getting us deep discounts warranted by the large quantities we were ordering.

"What are you guys doing with all this stuff?" a distributor asked Titi one day.

It might have been an innocent question. But the beauty and hair industry was small, and we did not want to make too much noise about what we were doing. We feared that they would get ideas and take our market share. Being set up in business already, they'd have a head start.

Hiring Tips

1. Small businesses can be overwhelmed easily when business grows, so make sure you have enough hands on deck.
2. When bringing new people into an organization, check their actions and attitudes to ensure that they're the right fit.
3. Ask yourself: Are they quick to step up and help before being asked? Are they polite and respectful? Is there an obvious enthusiasm?
4. Of course, check their references and consider their skill sets and experience, but remember, it's the intangibles that matter most. Individual character and integrity should be the most important items on your checklist when you're considering which employees to bring on board.

"Oh, people just really like it," Titi replied, keeping it vague. She'd usually feign some excuse to put them off or duck the question. In the end, they were not overly invested, because they were being paid immediately. The demand became huge, and it was clear we could not continue making this stuff in our basement. It got us thinking about finding a chemist to help us reverse-engineer the formula. That way, we could start getting it made by a contract manufacturer, like normal companies do.

Our decision to come up with our own proprietary formula was a brilliant move. Rather than giving the formula to a contract manufacturer, hiring a chemist would ensure that Miss Jessie's officially owned the rights to the recipe.

Since we were children, our father had drummed into us the importance of owning your stuff. He exposed us to artists like Ray Charles, who owned the rights to his music, and Madam C. J. Walker, who had patented her own hair formulas. He also told us many cautionary tales about talented people who lost everything because they had failed to establish ownership.

Ownership is key. Why do all that work only to risk losing everything to imitators with bigger resources?

By the time Titi and I were running our own business, the value of ownership was ingrained in us. The nineties were a time when many black entrepreneurs were first to market products and stake their claims: Carl Jones with Cross Colours, Puffy with Bad Boy record company, and Hype Williams with Beautiful Music Video, to name a few. We wanted to do the same in our untapped niche market.

Most upstart beauty companies never think to protect their intellectual property. But patents ultimately meant that we could never be held hostage by the maker, and we could take our business to another contract manufacturer if we were not happy with quality control or production costs. My paranoia about people stealing our ideas ran deep, which was why I insisted upon owning trademarks on all aspects of our business. I understood that what we had was valuable. Unique. Knowing this, Titi was smart enough to fill out the trademark paperwork every time we came out with a new product. This was long before any lawyer got involved, adding considerably to the value of our business.

Finding the right chemist was a challenge. We didn't even know where to begin. Consumer manufacturing wasn't our world, and we didn't have any contacts to speak of. It's not as if our competitors were about to share their production secrets. But we were determined. We ended up taking a two-hour drive to the home offices for an ingredient we used. We cased the place, going so far as to sift through their garbage to see if there was any kind of paperwork to reveal who they worked with to make the ingredient. There was nothing more than a big warehouse, but the size of the operation told us something.

"Miko, this could really be a huge business!" Titi realized when we came back from our snooping trip. "I mean, more than we ever imagined."

"What makes you think so?" I asked her.

"Because they're not even making the stuff at that location. It's just a facility for storing and distributing. Just imagine how much product they are shipping and how many people are buying the stuff."

Women in this country spend over $400 billion a year on beauty products, and the black hair and cosmetic industry sees sales of about $9 billion a year, according to the Black Owned Beauty Supply Association. Maybe, just maybe, we could get a piece of this.

My sister and I racked our brains, trying to think of someone who might be able to help us. Prior to the formulation of Curly Pudding, we had traveled to Chicago, where a lot of manufacturing for African-American hair-care products took place.

It was a disappointing trip. Although we'd been fortunate enough to make contact with one of the owners, who agreed to meet with us, he was blunt about what he could do for us within our tight budget. From what we saw and tested among the samples on the factory's shelves, nothing it was already producing came close to what we had in mind. The manufacturer claimed he could produce a prototype of the kind of crème-based curly-hair product we were aiming for, but all he ever sent us was another variation on conditioner.

The fact that we found no one who could make anything to our desired standards was a godsend. It inspired us to put together our own formulation—exactly what Miss Jessie would have done under the circumstances. "If they don't have what you want, make it yourself," she always told us.

After searching for and finally getting a referral from a fragrance manufacturer, we made contact with someone who could help us. We spent the next year with this chemist, reverse-engineering our ingredients to create a recipe that could be mass-produced. We went through a lot of trial and error to get our rudimentary formula exactly right.

PRODUCT EXTENSIONS

★

It wasn't just the formula for Curly Pudding that we had to figure out. By 2006, we had four products for curly hair: Curly Pudding, Curly Meringue, Curly Buttercreme, and Baby Buttercreme. I insisted we come up with Curly Meringue about three months after Curly Pudding, to give our customers more choice. Using our first product on every single type of curl was not the way to go. Not everything was for everyone. This formulation was a cousin to Curly Pudding, designed for a less tight curl.

Our styling products balanced hold factor while counteracting frizz by adding moisture. They were subtle differences, but the changes we made were intuitive, as a result of working with a variety of curl types in the salon. Because black women's hair is typically a lot drier, the more hold you have, the crunchier the hair will feel. We counterbalanced this with conditioning. Looser curl types, on the other hand, can take more hold without the curl looking too dry and crispy, and that was good for customers who wanted their styling to last a little longer. We also made Curly Meringue look and smell different, in a creamy yellow color with a piña colada fragrance that smelled good enough to eat.

A few months after that, we diversified with moisturizers—the Buttercremes—which could be used on their own or in combination with other styling products. People usually bought both. Curly Buttercreme was an immediate hit. We spiked this super-softening soufflé with cooling peppermint essence. Our customers loved it for growing out natural hair and preventing peppercorn-tangled knotted ends. It tamed hairline edges, moisturized pony puffs, and allowed for ease of at-home styling using two-strand twists, coils, braids, and cornrows. Clients with especially tight, curly, or kinky hair, as well as Transitioners—women who were growing out their processed hair—used it daily, quickly making it one of our best sellers. Although many women loved the tingling scalp sensation, I felt we needed a gentler option, so we came up with a lighter, less strongly scented version, Baby Buttercreme, which was also more child-friendly—although over half of the customers are adults, who use it for natural styling and daily moisturizing.

SPREADING THE WORD

★

As we diversified, we became more sophisticated about how we promoted ourselves. Realizing that the target market—women who had embraced their natural hair—did not typically go to salons, we decided from the beginning not to do what most hair product companies do: sell through salons. Instead, our conversation with our customer was direct, through our website. By 2005, we could afford to invest a little more in solidifying our reputation as market leaders for curly hair. We hired a publicist we found randomly online who had just opened her business. She got us into every major fashion and lifestyle magazine: *Glamour, WWD, O, Elle, Marie Claire, Allure, Ebony, Essence, New York, OK*, and *Nylon*.

We were adamant that we wouldn't target only magazines

for women of color. This had to be a broad-based marketing campaign. As a result, Miss Jessie's was quick to reso-
nate with all women who had
curly-hair needs, just as white
girls were our first salon customers when we got that ink in
Time Out. Somehow, the mainstream acceptance helped us to
win over some of the diehards
in the natural-hair movement.

> *Self-promotion is not only a good thing, it is required. It helps customers identify with the people behind the brand and saves a fortune on advertising costs.*

Alongside the media coverage, we were also getting recognition from top celebrity stylists. One of our earliest cham-
pions was Anthony Dickey. He was the gentleman at Louis
Licari's salon who recommended our products, helping us to
generate our first big wave of orders. They ordered our products for years and helped us to sustain our business.

RETAIL BREAKTHROUGH

★

The retail chain Ricky's had just started to carry us—our first
major retail distributor, with twenty-five stores. We approached
the chain about carrying our products because, although they
had a good selection of salon-level hair care, there was a glaring
omission in their product range. Titi and I went to the SoHo
Broadway store near Houston Street with my five-year-old in
tow. At the time there were only about two curly brands in
Ricky's, and those brands catered to a looser curl, so I thought
they needed our product on their shelves. While my son played

on the dirty trafficked floor with his trucks, Titi and I bum-rushed the stock guy and demanded to know why they didn't carry Miss Jessie's.

"Okay, no doubt, I'll try to hook you up," he told us, accepting our product samples to give to the store manager for the weekly Tuesday meeting at Ricky's headquarters.

A week later, we got the call that we were in. It was the start of a brand-new curly category in New York City. Ricky's quickly demanded as much product as we could produce. Demand was high. They couldn't keep us in stock, and trying to fulfill the orders was making us batty. This was true for all the smaller brick-and-mortar stores carrying our products.

We ran out of room in our basement for all the barrels of ingredients, which we had to keep in a storage locker on Hall Street in the Brooklyn Navy Yard. Titi used to drive up there with our new minivan stuffed to the gills. We were all busy worker bees, loading and unloading deliveries and shipments with our production guy and a few of the girls who helped out in our salon. My sister and I had never been so fit in our lives!

In addition to our Herculean efforts to get our product out to stores, we also worked hard to maintain control of presentation. Whenever we negotiated with beauty suppliers to carry our products, they had to send us photos of the inside and outside of their store. For us, it was important that we were not seen in a dingy location with poor merchandising and shelf placement. A lousy location could hurt the brand. As a result, we were highly selective about which stores we would allow to stock our jars and tubes of styling cream, gels, and conditioners.

PRESSURE COOKER

★

After the Ricky's deal, it became apparent that our product line could really take off. We were consumed with anxiety that we could suddenly get the call from a thousand stores and our lack of capacity would cause us to miss a huge opportunity. We were also paranoid that people would find out that we were making our products in our house. Doing all this street-style, putting the product together and hoping for the best, was keeping us up at night with what Miss Jessie called "worriation."

Business was booming, but all of the pressure was taking its toll. My sister and I found ourselves out of sync. The signs were showing of two people who worked way too closely together. By necessity, we'd been up under each other for a few years—ever since we'd moved to Bed-Stuy from downtown Brooklyn—and it wasn't healthy for our relationship. We were living, breathing, and sleeping Miss Jessie's. There was no room in our lives for anything else, and, due to the situation we'd faced in our last salon downtown, we barely left the house. My anger and resentment over that incident lingered for two years while I worked to get us to a profitable place. Driven as I was to get us past this rough patch, there was little respite outside of work. Rebuilding a business from zero left no room for having fun and socializing. We were toiling morning, noon, and night. It had to be that way to push past the frightening period of having had nothing, six years earlier.

Everything happened so fast for me. I went from being the

talent to being the businessperson in one swipe, without any warning or preparation. Meanwhile, my sister and I had never really dealt with the emotional aftermath of that earlier disappointment.

For two solid years after fleeing to Bed-Stuy, I was not pleased with Titi. I was a single parent feeling frustrated that we had lost our business downtown. It was mandatory for me to get back to work in our home salon to pay that month's mortgage. It was also an afterthought that ten days prior I'd delivered my son

Communicate, communicate, communicate. False expectations and frustrations can occur when you don't make intentions clear.

through a cesarian section surgery, and was walking around with staples holding my stomach together. I went into repair mode and neglected to fully resolve the issues. As a consequence, Titi got the full brunt of my fury.

The tension between us continued until we hired some help in 2002. By 2005, we were able to hire more employees. I was relieved that we had built our business back up and had gotten to a point where my sister's role could be heavily reduced, with employees to carry that load.

In June 2006, we moved the entire production business to a warehouse at 43 Hall Street, not far from where we had the storage unit. For forty-five hundred dollars a month, we got five thousand square feet—all the storage space we needed—and a loading dock, which simplified the logistics of our business. No more rolling individual heavy barrels down those narrow three cement steps on our garden floor. Now the UPS truck could back up onto it, and we could take all our deliveries without the prying eyes of our neighbors or the heavy pressure on our backs. A few months later, our formulas were ready, and we were able to move our production to a contract manufacturer. Our business was finally coming up from underground. We were no longer a basement operation.

It would have been a huge relief except for one thing: As soon as we moved our production business out of the brownstone, Titi decided to run the Miss Jessie's product company by herself, cutting me out completely.

They say you should never mix business with family. I disagree, because together Titi and I had created something wonderful, and that kind of achievement could have happened only through the passion, devotion, and love we shared as siblings. They also say blood is thicker than water. The problem is, blood is also messier.

Over the years, as we poured all of our energy and time into building the business, we'd drifted apart. Resentments on both sides ran deep. Other than matters of work, we barely communicated. I was faced with a sobering reality: I was sued and iced out of Miss Jessie's by Titi for the next two years.

There had been rumblings. Miss Jessie's was in the process of reformatting operating agreements and organizing them into LLCs, and that was raising some questions about who had contributed what to the business. But this whole time, I had left the operational side of the business, including paperwork and contracts, to Titi. Immersed in rebuilding our new salon and product business with a focus on curly hair, I hadn't been paying attention to the details. When I asked to see our company's bank records, Titi responded by withdrawing her half of the money.

Titi's lawyer's letter was like a sucker punch to the gut. It categorically stated that Titi had sole control of the business, which was technically untrue. Years earlier, we had named Titi manager on the boilerplate partnership agreement we'd purchased from Staples. Though that did not mean I had less ownership, it gave Titi more power on paper, which neither of us understood when we signed the paperwork. A judge, reviewing the documents, agreed and ordered me to give up all the money in our joint business bank account. All I had worked for, everything I had built over the years, was taken away by court order.

Adding to the insult, I was told I was to continue working at the salon for a salary of three hundred dollars a week. Of course I refused. There was nothing in the contract that required me to stay, although I was not allowed to provide hair

Tips for Family Businesses

1. Try to compartmentalize; keep work and personal feelings separate. This is a tough one in a family business, where personal tensions can infect the day-to-day operations.
2. Always put the interests of the business first, or family arguments could cost you in time, energy, and lost income.
3. Remember, emotions can wreak havoc on your bottom line.

services anywhere within a hundred miles of New York—a noncompete that Titi and her lawyer insisted upon enforcing.

I was deeply hurt by the blindside, and shocked that it was coming from my big sister. From fights in the schoolyard to raising my son, Titi had always been my staunchest protector and most dedicated helpmate. This was not supposed to happen.

The circumstance prompted me to relocate my salon business to Washington, D.C., where I commuted weekly, leaving my son with a sitter every Thursday morning until I could return on Saturday night. Luckly, my salon staff came with me, commuting back and forth along I-95. We quickly built up a thriving salon business. In addition to my old clients, many of whom followed me to D.C. to maintain their hair, there was a sizeable untapped market of women in the area who were starving for our naturally-curly-hair services.

In many ways, it was a learning opportunity. I had always left the operations side of the business to Titi. Anything that had to do with management or administration, I'd delegated to her. But in D.C., I had no choice. I had to do all my own paperwork. I had to put myself in charge of the scheduling, budgeting, incorporating, training, ordering supplies, and cracking down on product theft. I was a solo act, dealing directly with staff, suppliers, graphic and website designers, and clients. I was managing three assistants at a time, often remotely from New York. I had to be fully accountable to myself, with no room for excuses, blame, or guilt about my exacting standards and no-nonsense management style. All of this practical, hands-on experience made me a more well-rounded and confident businesswoman. More important, it made me fearless.

However, running a business so far away from home was incredibly stressful, as was leaving behind my crying son each week. Driving back to New York one winter night along the Beltway, I was so fatigued that my car spun out of control. Thank God a huge truck was on the side of the road to block my car from going over the edge of the overpass.

Always plan for success. Stay busy building something, no matter what is happening in your business. Time is valuable. Use it to learn, grow, and improve.

On and on it went. After a year, we reconciled and planned to stop the lawsuit, until Titi pulled out at the last minute. Back to D.C. I went. This time, my salon staff members were done with the commuting, so I had to start hiring local assistants to help with the workload. The grind was relentless, but I needed the money to pay for my lawyer. Furious at my sister, I was determined to fight her with every fiber of my being. I knew it was going to be a rough battle, and the legal costs could bleed me dry, but I couldn't live with myself if I allowed Titi to take my business from me like that. My blood and sweat was tied up with Miss Jessie's. It was who I was; it was my son's future. Giving in would devalue all that I had struggled to build. For the sake of my self-respect, I had to go to war with my own sister.

SIDING WITH THE TRUTH

★

It was one of the worst periods of our lives. My sister and I could have lost everything that we'd built together. I couldn't

help but think none of this would have happened if Miss Jessie
had been alive. She always sided with the truth, and she would
have wasted no time telling us we were family.

Miss Jessie never would have allowed that lawsuit to take
place. For her, it was always family first, ever since she saw
the way her sister was mistreated by her stepfather all those
years ago. So imagine her reaction to litigation between her two
grandbabies. She'd have turned over in her grave.

I never missed my grandmother more.

Nine

* * *

A SUDDEN TWIST

A change is gonna come.

—SAM COOKE

It was a warm, early summer day in June 2008, and we were hoping for a thaw in our cold war. The feud had already lasted two years, and a judge finally ordered us to mediate. Titi and I decided to meet at my lawyer's office in Lower Manhattan to talk about a settlement. After rarely spending a day apart in over thirty-six years of living, we'd become virtual strangers, and this would be the first time we'd met face-to-face in months. Despite the sunshine outside, the climate inside that conference room was freezing.

I'd been dreading this moment. I was so angry that I couldn't trust what I'd do to my sister when we got in a room together; I had visions of myself physically hurting her. As I took my seat, I grabbed the armrests so tightly that my knuckles were turning white; I feared that if I loosened my grip, my fists would start flying. But I kept thinking about what Miss Jessie always told me: "Miko, use your common sense!"

We were trying to decide whether to dissolve the company or have Titi buy out my shares and take over completely. While it made no sense to close down a business that was clearly in the black, Miss Jessie's was my vision, my heart, and my soul, and I couldn't see the business moving forward without me. As far as I was concerned, I could not live with myself if I did not fight to win back what I had built for my son.

We went at it for two hours, haggling about who brought what to our business and exactly what each contribution was worth. I couldn't see how it was even possible to parse any of it out, because until the lawsuit happened, we'd been completely intertwined, each giving 100 percent of ourselves. We had been a tight little unit, and I'd have trusted her with my life. Titi and I had been together on everything; she was even coparent to my son.

As everyone was talking, I thought, *This is bullshit!* It was clear that my sister was just spouting whatever she was being fed by that lawyer of hers. She was barely able to make eye contact with me as she sat motionless in her seat. When she accidentally caught my glance, she had no light in her eyes, as if the girl I knew had retreated inside herself, with no real connection to anything she was saying. I was suddenly sad for her—something was wrong with this picture. But my fury was greater than any observation I'd made. She was in the middle of telling her story in a way that supported her claim when I lost it: "Titi, why the fuck are you lying? You can't even hold a straight face, talking that bullshit!"

"Don't talk to my client," Titi's lawyer said. As far as he was concerned, the case was airtight. As long as Titi stuck to her story, he was about to make a nice chunk of change on his fees, in addition to all the money he had already made off of our company. But I wasn't having it.

Someone called for a time-out, and Titi and I took a bathroom break, away from the lawyers. Behind the closed doors of the ladies' room, we had a long talk and finally reconciled.

For two years, Titi had been clinically depressed, isolated from our family, and barely functioning at work. She was tired and had lost the will to fight anymore. My rage melted into compassion, and we hugged it out.

Just like that, the war was over. Titi made the decision to end the lawsuit then and there. In the stipulation, we agreed that Titi would drop 1 percent of her share in the company to 49 percent, giving me ultimate control. It offered us some much-needed clarity.

PARTNERS IN CRIME

★

If anything good had come out of this lawsuit, it was the fact that our estrangement forced us to see ourselves as individuals, independent of each other. Before this, we didn't know where one of us ended and the other began. It was necessary to do an honest self-evaluation and carve out our separate identities.

A clearer understanding of our individual strengths could

help us become better partners, which is crucial when two people are running a business together. Miss Jessie had always understood the importance of being part of a duo, from the time she took in her baby stepsister, Aunt Sis. The two lived together, raising my grandmother's four children and Aunt Sis's two kids in the same apartment, pooling their scant resources to survive without any husbands and fathers on the scene. They managed their household like a small business, buying groceries and paying for heat, shelter, and clothing for their family. They even played the numbers together, sharing in the winnings.

Most of all, they had each other's back. They got physical if they felt someone in the family was being threatened. Once, when Miss Jessie's number hit and the numbers man came to the door to try to stiff her out of the money owed to her, Aunt Sis went to Miss Jessie's aid and they gave him a beating he never forgot, throwing him down the stairs of their walk-up apartment. They told him there'd be more of the same if he didn't bring them their money that day.

That was the nature of my partnership with Titi before the lawsuit. Even when we weren't getting along, no one could say anything to us about the other. The problems we may have had were between us, and we wouldn't tolerate a third party tearing the other down. Together, we were always a united front.

Put it in black and white. Getting things in writing takes out the guesswork, assumptions, and false expectations, allowing each party to play his or her position.

We'd been naive when we entered into our official business partnership years before. We should have handled paperwork through an attorney and meticulously spelled out each person's role in the organization. Instead, we took a costly shortcut with a boilerplate agreement that didn't reflect the true nature of our partnership. The document was rudimentary, and it left a wide gap for misinterpretation, which, along with our personal communication breakdown, led to disaster. But we'd learned our lesson: Partnerships are tricky unless everyone understands who does what, and that's especially true when you're in business with family.

TOGETHER AGAIN

Nobody had won; we'd just made our lawyers richer. Attorneys add value to a business when it comes to making deals and drawing up contracts, but they have no business in relationships. We learned that lesson the hard way. But as we walked out of that office, we felt like a huge weight had lifted. Finally, the ordeal was over, and we had each other back in our lives. Being apart like that never felt right. We went back to Titi's apartment in Brooklyn.

"Miko, will you please stay with me tonight?"

"Of course, Titi. I'm here for you!"

Titi didn't want to spend another day alone, and honestly, I was worried about her. The guilt and pain had taken their toll on my big sister, and it was time for me to be *her* rock. We still had a lot of healing to do, but Titi and I recognized that

Your business is bigger than you. Set aside personal grievances for the greater good of the enterprise.

there was something much bigger at stake: our love for each other. We were always better together than we were apart. Miss Jessie's was a sister act. That was how we'd shaped every aspect of our business from day one. We were in this together because we chose to be, and not just because we were related. Separately, each of us had the wherewithal to succeed. But together, we could continue to build something much greater than its parts.

TAKING STOCK

★

Titi asked me to come back to Miss Jessie's. I agreed to shut down my salon in D.C. to work with the product company at the warehouse on Hall Street five days a week, continuing my work in the Bed-Stuy salon on weekends. We needed to do everything we could to build our business back up.

After two years, we'd lost some market share, and our business was stagnant. By 2007, competitors were surfacing. The good news was that the business was still profitable, with revenues growing from $1.7 million in 2006 to $3.2 million in 2008, subsisting off existing clientele and reorders.

Our own tight fiscal management also saved us. "Neither a borrower nor a lender be," Miss Jessie used to say, quoting Shakespeare, and we took it to heart. We had no debt and always paid our bills on time. I know it goes against everything people say you should do when

Always pay your bills on time. Suppliers will remember being well treated and will stick by you when times are tough.

managing your payables—you're supposed to send out that check as late as possible to hang on to the interest—but as soon as an invoice came through our door, we paid it. As a service-oriented business, we wanted to treat others the way we liked to be treated, never making others wait for their money. The result was a rock-solid relationship with our vendors and suppliers, who were willing to give us deeper pricing discounts because they knew they'd always get paid on time.

Growing up in a home where money was always tight, and watching our father make it only to spend it all again and then some, was arguably one of the most enduring lessons we learned about business. For all his independence, Daddy really didn't have his own, and seeing him cycle in and out of debt made Titi and me extremely careful with our pennies. We never wanted to overextend ourselves. We weren't cheap, and we took care of the people we loved, but we never wanted to be in a situation where we didn't have complete control and freedom to take the business to the next level without being beholden to the bank.

That salon move on Bond Street was another lesson learned. By moving into the house in Bed-Stuy, we'd gotten rid of the overhead of a fifteen-hundred-dollar monthly rental and given ourselves a nice big tax write-off. Every dollar we made went toward paying down the mortgage and covering our bills. Our partnership had been 50/50, but it all went into the same pool of money, which we put in a savings account at the bank. Even

Cut costs with surgical precision so that you can afford to invest in the employees, equipment, marketing, or capacity necessary to grow your business.

when we had built enough of a cushion, we gave ourselves modest salaries and kept the bulk of what we made in a savings account. We didn't go out and party, like many successful single women in their early thirties. We shared a car, shoes, bags, beauty products, you name it. And that was how we lived, even when we were bringing in high six figures in net profits.

Being frugal just came naturally to us—something we learned from Miss Jessie. But she also taught us the difference between "penny wise and pound foolish." Our grandmother didn't have much in the way of resources, but she never skimped. She negotiated, she cut corners, and she stretched a dollar, but she would never be cheap for its own sake. What she did have, she knew how to spend. She'd go to the supermarket and buy that big box of Tide detergent, because she knew she had a lot of children's clothes to wash, and in her experience, that brand was the best for getting the job done. She invested in the economy size because it saved her time in the form of an extra trip to the store, and money, because bulk is always better if it's something you know you are going to use a lot. She taught us that while it's necessary to economize, you must always invest in your priorities.

We must have absorbed that lesson well because, at every level, our lifestyle was self-contained and carefully managed. It revolved around the salon and the business, which was our hearth, our home, our security, our livelihood, and our family. That house on Hancock Street was like a fortress, and we guarded what we had and ran things with military precision.

This enabled us to reinvest in our product business on an as-needed basis. The year Curly Pudding came on the market, 2004, was the same year we paid off our Hancock Street mortgage in full. We hadn't ever taken out business loans, financing the product company entirely through the proceeds from the salon, and keeping overheads low in a high-margin business. I was also adamant about never paying full price for anything.

Throughout the building of Miss Jessie's, this approach allowed us to take some risks. Cash flow, or lack of it, stops many small enterprises from making their next best move. But not having to live hand to mouth and knowing the bills would be paid gave us the courage to follow our instincts about pricing and business expansion. Cash kept piling up because, after all of our operating and living expenses, there was a net profit at the end of each month that was continually rising.

Although we were careful about spending, we were in tune with the business and knew precisely the right time to grow. That was why we bought new equipment and insisted on hiring people to handle customer orders, pack boxes, and send out shipments. We could physically feel when it was becoming too much. Although we still operated with a tight budget, we kept finding little ways to make it easier and accommodate our rapid growth.

That laser focus on our bottom line protected us. Not only did it keep us from going under during our litigation, it gave us a cushion when the recession hit in 2008, and it bought us the time we needed to get our operations flowing efficiently again.

BIG-GIRL PANTIES

★

The fact was that we'd been coasting for too long, and it was time to take back some control. When Titi and I got back together as business partners, we were far from where we needed to be. A start-up in a burgeoning new market should have had much better sales growth, but we were losing ground to cheaper copycats. During our time apart, the business had lost its direction and its status as a leader and product innovator.

Although the suit had been emotionally and financially draining, it made me more skillful as a manager. Understanding exactly what needed to be done to rehabilitate Miss Jessie's, I wasted no time implementing the same rules and structure in the warehouse that we had at the salon in the early days. To make up for lost ground, I pursued more retail partnerships, developed new marketing campaigns, built a new website, and followed through on existing relationships to let our customers know that Miss Jessie's was back.

There were a lot of cracks to repair. That said, Titi had made some smart moves while I was away from the business. She'd recognized the potential for the Atlanta market and found a retailer to introduce Miss Jessie's to these customers. Understanding that many retail customers would find it hard to digest Miss Jessie's fifty-eight-dollar price point for the professional-size product, Titi, who had developed considerable marketing expertise in my absence, also launched an annual "buy one, get one free" promotion, or BOGO. It was an ingenious way to introduce the product to more spendthrift fans and help build a loyal following, and it's a tradition that we've continued over the years in some form or other. Titi called it a "sampling opportunity." It worked well because it got our

Sales and promotions, strategically placed and timed, are good for business.

products into more hands and brought in a healthy profit, which we reinvested in the business for the upcoming year.

In my absence, Titi had also hired more people. She got the subcontract manufacturing underway, and kept the distribution, packaging, and shipping side of our product business humming. As the product business grew, she realized the need for better infrastructure to manage our partnerships, contractors, and employees. We'd been flying by the seat of our pants, and it was leading to mistakes on the fulfillment side of the business. Titi invested in a computer system that helped us communicate and keep track of orders. It became a key building block for Miss Jessie's back-office operations.

But then Titi faded from view, barely showing her face in the warehouse. It was time for a fresh start.

Ten

TRANSITIONERS

The best think you can do is the right thing;
the next best thing you can do is the wrong thing;
the worst think you can do is nothing.

—THEODORE ROOSEVELT

One of the hardest things for a small-business owner to do is fire people. There were more than a few bad apples in the bunch but there's a tendency to hang on to those who were there from the early days out of a sense of loyalty, even when they have not grown along at the same pace with you. But we didn't have the luxury of holding on to what wasn't working for us. As we rebuilt, we needed to decide quickly who should stay and who should go.

Fortunately, my sister had hired a couple of solid employees. Titi told me about one employee in particular who had lots of potential. She had not been able to give him her attention over the past year, so she asked me if I could put his creativity and good intentions to use. After meeting Antonio, I could see we had a gem.

Titi had hired him in December 2006, about a year into the start of our product company, to help out with packaging and shipping. Antonio had been struggling to find work when he saw our ad on Craigslist. He applied, even though the position was beneath his experience in customer service and computer systems. When he showed up for his interview, Titi could sense his potential right away. His references were glowing. It was clear that he was a worker.

Like us, he'd been independent from an early age. Titi especially liked the fact that he started off their conversation by quoting the Chilean poet Pablo Neruda. Here was another creative type to add to our orbit. He began working at our Hall Street warehouse the very evening Titi interviewed him.

My sister and I share an instinct for people that we inherited from our grandmother. Miss Jessie was always a shrewd judge of character. She could size you up in a heartbeat. She didn't need résumés to tell her the people she had time for. Where people went to school, where they came from, what they looked like, or what culture and ethnicity they were a part of made no difference to her. Honesty, loyalty, and a strong work ethic—these were the things she cared about most in a person.

We watched her dealings with people closely, whether meeting folks who came through our house or shopping at the supermarket. Afterward, she used to tell us, "That one is going to have a hard time in life" or "I'd slow that one down when talking to make sure they don't try to slide one in." Miss Jessie was even a filter for some of the friends we brought over.

"Don' trust that one, Miko," Miss Jessie told me after I'd introduced her to one of my new friends from the neighborhood. "She's bad news."

Sure enough, the girl stole money from me. Miss Jessie was always right.

For the most part, when we were hiring on a hunch, we got it right, too. Of course, we interviewed carefully, asking probing questions and paying just as much attention to attitude and body language as we did to applicants' words. But we weren't interested in a laundry list of qualifications. A small consumer-product business doesn't necessarily need a bunch of employees with MBAs or strong pedigrees. We needed people who were passionate about what we did, eager for a chance to prove themselves, and willing to try anything. Skills and experience counted, but members of our team needed to share our entrepreneurial spirit and drive. I can learn about a potential employee or business partner during the course of negotiating compensation and benefits. For example, if a potential employee's first question and primary concern is the number of sick or vacation days, then I am likely to pass and move on to the next candidate. Not that those matters are not important—they are—but I am more impressed when a potential employee wants to know about opportuni-

When hiring, look for integrity, loyalty, and a willingness to work hard. These qualities are worth a hundred MBAs.

ties for growth within the company. In addition, when I am selecting a potential business partner, I try to discern whether the prospective partner is interested in building a relationship or simply wants a short courtship with a quick and sometimes expensive payout. To get additional insight, I frequently ask all new hires and partners to suggest their own compensation. I know my budget and limitations, and I do not want to insult or devalue anyone's worth. If the salary or compensation is just too high, then there is no point in negotiating. Even if a person or partner would accept less compensation, I cannot imagine being happy in a postion that pays less than you wanted and what you thought you were worth. In the end, that person will not be happy or will be constantly looking for the next opportunity. And that's bad for my business. When done properly, an interview can tell you a lot about a candidate's experiences and capabilities as well as the candidate's character and motivation for wanting to be a part of the team. Whether Antonio, for example, was packing boxes or working with me in our marketing department or executing our work on labels and billboards or managing the salon floor, he applied himself.

We hired another gem in April 2005, when we were still running the product business out of our brownstone. I needed someone to answer the phone—someone with good manners and a pleasant tone. In a business like ours, first impressions count, and you'd be amazed at how hard it is to find someone who knows good phone etiquette. I tried one college student on the phones for about ten minutes, and that was all it took for me to tell she was one of us.

Fiona had been raised by her grandmother in the British Virgin Islands until she moved to Crown Heights, Brooklyn, at sixteen, to be with her mother. She was soft-spoken and respectful, with a Caribbean lilt that made her perfect for customer service. I especially liked her old-school manners. But again, it was her work ethic that got us. She was putting herself through college at Baruch while working two jobs. As soon as she graduated, we offered her a full-time job.

Today, having taken additional college courses to improve her skills and better herself, Fiona works in accounts payable. We have a handful of dedicated young employees who have been with us for the whole journey, growing in skills and responsibilities. They all have one thing in common: They have never said no to a task we set for them. They share our DNA of resourcefulness and willingness to do whatever it takes to get

> *Your employees' public demeanor and phone etiquette say something about your brand. They represent you, so hold them to the highest standards.*

the job done. And they are fiercely loyal. It's why Miss Jessie's is more like an extended family than a regular place of business. We trust each other and have complete confidence that when we give someone a task or responsibility, there is simply no time for excuses as to why something was not done. You would never hear any of these employees say, "That's not in my job description." They enjoy being given new challenges and always rise to the occasion. As the product business started to grow, we placed Fiona in charge of our shipping department, handling everything but packing the boxes. Her gentle demeanor belied a tough streak, because there were a lot of different personalities to manage, or as she put it, "crazy people you might not even talk to in the street."

CLEANING HOUSE

★

When I came back from my forced hiatus, it was time to bring in additional staff. We needed to bring in someone to identify where we were being inefficient. To that end, we brought in my old college friend Augustus. He had been working in the banking industry for a while, doing training classes and working with the CFO of a large organization. He was someone who understood the creative side of our business and was also familiar with standard business practices. Best of all, he was stern.

We wasted no time making our operations more streamlined and efficient. We put everyone at our 43 Hall Street location under the microscope. We drilled down into all of our business functions, including order fulfillment, packaging, and shipping. It was like a deep audit of our operations, enabling us to spot the leaks, identify the communication breakdowns, and figure out who was right for what position, who was willing to grow, and who was not. Then we cleaned house—something a lot of small businesses fail to do as they transition to the next level. Think of it as a kind of Big Chop for healthier growth.

One of our most important realizations from this "taking stock" was that we were spending far too much time and too many resources on taking and processing orders. On one level, it was a good sign that we had too much business to handle under one roof. By 2007, we had

Fire people when you must. Sometimes it's necessary to make painful cuts to payroll for the long-term health of your business.

more than ten products we were shipping to tens of thousands of customers around the world. We were used to being hands-on for everything, and keeping all our business functions in-house to ensure everything was done right, and it was hard to give up control.

We liked to work only with partners we trusted, and out-sourcing such a huge part of our operations was scary. In the end, we realized that we were a product company, not a shipping and distribution center. We canvassed several different distribution channels until we found the right fit, putting someone reliable in charge of fulfillment and customer care.

It was a tough decision to make, because there are inherent risks when you take something off the premises and are no longer in complete control of how things are handled. At first we had problems with the way the products were delivered. Items sometimes arrived damaged because there wasn't enough stuffing in the box. Other times it was the wrong product. We also had issues with late deliveries and theft. When we started shipping to customers, we were using Miss Jessie's–branded packaging. People were so desperate to get their hands on our product that they were pulling it off the back of the delivery trucks! It was incredibly flattering that our products were being coveted in this way, but also costly. Our solution was to use plain packaging, and the complaints stopped.

Miss Jessie's is an affordable luxury, and our customers and retail partners have the right to expect a certain level of service. We put someone on it internally to follow up with the fulfill-ment company whenever there was a problem. If a customer was unhappy about a parcel arriving late or damaged, for example, we would overnight it to her, but that was the extent of the shipping we handled ourselves.

This move freed us to concentrate on what we do best: marketing and product development. The natural-hair business had exploded in the previous two years, with more brands clamoring for attention in the category, and bloggers playing a bigger role in the natural-hair space. In an increasingly crowded marketplace, we had to get aggressive, with more print ads, a new website, and hair shows. We also made a push to expand our geographical footprint.

Don't be afraid to outsource. Concentrate your energies and expertise in areas of the business that will reap the maximum benefit.

One of the first things we did was refocus on the Atlanta market. I had a friend living down there, Christine, the woman who had blessed me with the bartending gig all those years ago. It was time to pay her a visit.

DIRTY SOUTH

★

When I arrived in January 2009, Christine picked me up at the airport, and I almost didn't recognize her as the foxy, go-getting girl I'd known in Brooklyn a decade earlier. Christine had had a successful corporate career in HR, but the recession had hit hard, and the company was forced to downsize. She'd been struggling for months to find a new job. In fact, she'd just sold her house because she could no longer cover her mortgage payments.

Everything about Christine's demeanor suggested a woman in a state of defeat. Her shoulders were hunched, she had on no makeup, and she was dressed in sweats, as if she wasn't accustomed to leaving the house. I couldn't help but notice that her hair had been randomly cornrowed, with straight relaxed ends on the bottom and grays popping from the temples. Her look didn't reflect who she really was, because this was a girl who had always taken care of her appearance.

"Christine, remember when you helped me out that day?"

"What day?"

"You know, when you gave me the opportunity to bartend that party." I actually had to remind her of that kindness. "Well, now I am going to help you!"

"Help me?" she said, getting a kick out of the conversation and not really taking me seriously.

"Yes, Christine," I said.

I could show her better than tell her, so I started by doing her hair. I snipped off the straight ends to loosen her tightly coiled kinks into a chin-length cascade of ringlets, groomed with Curly Pudding and Baby Buttercreme. Then I took her shopping and got her a whole new outfit, along with a makeover at the MAC counter.

"Miko, you don't have to spend your money, I don't need no charity," she protested. "Just seeing you and spending time with you is enough to lift up my spirits."

As we were browsing through the lipsticks, a couple of women approached me. "Hey, aren't you that girl from Miss Jessie's?" one of them asked me, requesting a photo.

"Oh, my God!" Christine squealed. "What's going on? Your hair products have people in Atlanta knowing you like that?

Now, what have you been doing for the last ten years? Tell me everything, because last time I checked, you were doing a little hair and bartending for me!"

We both just about fell on the floor, laughing. In that moment, it was as if the previous decade of heartache and stress had just melted away. It was so good to see her and get back to the way we were all those years ago, when we were friends in Brooklyn without too much to worry about in life.

By the end of her head-to-toe makeover, Christine was looking like her foxy self again. I saw the sparkle and sass I remembered her having, and it gave me an idea. On that trip to Atlanta, Titi and I had planned to visit as many salons as we could, because we sensed something was wrong with our Atlanta partner. We went to Atlanta to scout out other distributors and retailers to diversify the business and found, as we suspected, that this partner was diverting the Miss Jessie's customer to new competitors.

Once we linked up with other salons and partners, we decided to introduce Miss Jessie's by doing some meet-and-greets, in addition to curl demonstrations in Atlanta, to personally connect with our customers. I needed an assistant to do a bit of everything, because we had our work cut out for us. Targeting stylists and doing hair shows wasn't our usual method for promoting Miss Jessie's, because most of our core customers—women who rocked their natural curls—did their own hair at home, and few salons besides ours had the knowledge or techniques to adequately cater to their needs. The existing situation with our partner forced us to come at it from all angles. Christine knew the city, so she could drive me around and make sure I hit all the right salons.

By the end of that day, it was as if Christine had caught the Miss Jessie's fever. It was a direct example of how Miss Jessie's empowers women. Christine's hair transformation was a first step toward getting her self-esteem back.

I began to gently talk to her about independence. My idea was for her to become her own boss and perhaps sell Miss Jessie's products, or maybe she should consider a career in hairstyling—she was always pretty good at it.

"You know, I think I can do this!" she told me. "Send a few cases of product to me, and let's see if I can sell them."

Within a few weeks, sales had blown up, and for a while Christine was reordering as many as two thousand units from us each month. She had become an entrepreneur, making a good living at something she loved.

Leverage local knowledge when possible. If you know and trust someone in a new market, give him or her a chance to open doors for you.

HIGH SCHOOL REUNION

★

A year later, in 2010, Titi and I decided we should go back to Atlanta to do a hair event with a local salon. The idea was people could come to us to try out samples and have us demonstrate some techniques, then make their purchases with the salon.

That Saturday the salon opened and it was like one big party, with the deejay we hired playing dance music, and trays of snacks and refreshments all laid out along with product samples, to give our visitors a taste of the Miss Jessie's spirit. We liked people to leave us with smiles on their faces.

Even though they're a lot of work, Titi and I love doing these events, because they allow us to really connect with our customers and see all the different hair types and get feedback on the Miss Jessie's stylers and conditioners that work best for them. We give away samples because we know they will be loved, and we demonstrate our products on a section of hair, wetting it down and styling it to show the before and after.

During the event, I could feel someone watching me. It was my old high school sidekick, Neal, who'd seen some news item about us online and decided to come and surprise me at the show. He hadn't changed one bit, except that he had his young son by his side.

MARKETING THROUGH MUSIC

As we caught up, Neal told me about all the other work he'd been doing in promotions. Ever since he'd been on the road with his rapper sister, Sweet Tee, he'd maintained his connection to the music industry, earning his living organizing huge concerts in Jamaica, Queens, as well as events for the Super Bowl and Mardi Gras. Neal understood the value of hitting the streets and building up personal contacts when you wanted to promote something. He used to do block parties in Queens long before the Internet existed.

It got me thinking about how, every time we did a hair show or ran an ad, our competitors followed our lead. We kept changing up our marketing approach, but we did not see the benefit of swimming in an overcrowded pool. But Neal was someone who could get our name out in spaces far beyond the naturally-curly-hair marketplace. I brought him in as a consultant.

Neal started by leveraging his music connections, getting our products out at jazz festivals and old-school concerts. He wanted to get samples in the hands of customers in the thirty-plus demographic who were going somewhere to have fun. Meanwhile, he was brazen about handing out Curly Pudding and Curly Buttercreme to celebrities. He'd spent his life around entertainers like Whitney Houston, Bobby Brown, the House-wives of Atlanta, and all the other entertainers who lived in his area, and he had no problem walking straight up to Jill Scott with a Miss Jessie's goodie bag.

Using his urban-music marketing training, Neal also got us in the news. When India Arie was making headlines based on allegations that she was bleaching her skin, he handed her a Miss Jessie's bag at the Phoenix Jazz Festival, and the press took pictures that landed on the website Media Take Out. Time and again, he made our product visible in the mainstream.

> *When everyone else goes right, go left. Unconventional paths to promotion will keep the competition guessing and potentially broaden your customer base.*

GRAB-AND-GO

★

This kind of promotion helped put our consumer product on the radar in a way that's much more organic and cost-effective than straight advertising. While we have never relied heavily on celebrity endorsements, mentions in the entertainment press get us into a broader national conversation.

But we were never starstruck. Titi and I were too busy to get caught up in the celebrity scene. While we understood the benefits of getting endorsements from high-profile people and handing out gift bags at red-carpet events, that task had its own potential hazards.

Our first such event, WEEN (Women in Entertainment Empowerment Network), held at the Hammerstein Ballroom in New York City, was a case in point. We'd set up a gift suite with bags of Miss Jessie's products to give to the stars as they were leaving. We had created a beautiful display table with vases that my mother had given me for good luck, and filled them with flower arrangements. My assistant Antonio was with me. We were being gracious to all the celebrities, making sure they got loaded up with Miss Jessie's gifts, when my assistant noticed that one of my son's favorite personalities, Lil Mama, a hip-hop recording artist from our beloved Brooklyn, was helping herself to not just the gift bags but also several of the vases. Though she could have had no idea what those vases meant and who had given them to us, she had her arms full of about four of them and was heading for the door. I asked Antonio to please apologize to her for the confusion but to get them back.

"Um, excuse me, Lil Mama," he said, catching up to her. The poor guy looked terrified.

"Yeah?" she said, turning around to face him.

"Uh, sorry, but those vases are just our props, not give-aways," he stammered.

"Nah, they were on the table with the other stuff left out, and they're mine now," she said.

Antonio came back empty-handed.

Although I would have loved to let her keep them, I just couldn't—my mother had given me those vases. I had to do a lightweight sprint to catch up to her, because she moved fast. I said, "Hi, I'm sorry—those were not the giveaways, so I need to get them back for our table."

"What are you gonna do?" she asked me. "Fight me for it?"

Before I knew it, I found myself gathering the vases from her arms and placing them behind me on a table. In that moment, I caught a look of pure mischief in her piercing green eyes. Clearly, she'd been joking. I was relieved that things were on a harmonious note, because I did not want my son to be disappointed if she were anything less than the classy young lady she turned out to be in that brief encounter.

FIRE-TESTED

★

At that point in my life, I was prepared to say no to anyone. After what I'd been through with Titi, my most formidable foe, nothing could scare me anymore. The noncompete that had forced me to work away from the tristate area, leaving my son behind during the week to build up a client base all over again, was rough. But it taught me a valuable lesson: No matter what happens, even if I lose everything, I will always have my two hands and my God-given talent. Take away from me everything I have built, and I will always be able to feed and support myself and my son. Knowing what I was capable of—on my own, without anyone's help—was incredibly empowering. It meant that I would never have to sell out. This freedom of entrepreneurship was the reason I'd gotten into business on my own in the first place. It was the source of my success, self-respect, and happiness. I could always be true to who I was and maintain the integrity of the Miss Jessie's name.

As the brand grew in popularity and profits, we were repeatedly approached by major retail chains that wanted to carry the Miss Jessie's products. The natural instinct is to say yes to every opportunity. But, by now, experience—not instinct—had taught me better. It seems odd, but doing business with certain chain stores, under certain conditions, would not add much value—at least not to me. After we calculated all the additional expenses and reviewed the chains' terms, it was clear profits would have been reed-thin and the frustration level would have been mile-high. If I could not get my terms—the terms that allowed me to run my business smoothly, then I would pass. I stood firm, refusing to compromise, not because I wanted to be difficult or demanding, but because I

Don't be afraid to say no to an opportunity. As long as you can cover your bills and be self-sustaining, there's no reason to accept what you know is less than you deserve.

did not know any other way to run my business successfully. I do not doubt that others might have agreed to certain terms or found a way to make the deal work, but I could not and would not pretend otherwise. So, I just said no and passed. Looking back, I see there must have been times when I left money on the table and missed out on good opportunities, but I do not have much, if any, regret at all. I am learning and growing more confident with each passing successful year that the truly good opportunities will present themselves again. And I will be ready to accept them.

Many young businesses are tempted by the large amount of up-front cash that can be one of the immediate benefits of doing business with a large distribution partner. But you have to consider the longer-term costs of such short-term gains. Those percentages could ultimately kill a business. Besides, there's power in saying no. It frees you up for the next opportunity. You just have to believe that something better will come along; if you continue to work hard to build your brand, it almost always does.

Eleven

* * *

BULL'S-EYE

*I'm a success today because I had a friend who believed
in me and I didn't have the heart to let him down.*

—ABRAHAM LINCOLN

It was the kind of email we tended to ignore. By 2009, we were used to getting all kinds of calls or emails with someone soliciting something. Most of them were nonsense, and very few materialized into anything, so if it was an address we didn't recognize, we routinely dismissed it. Our thoughtful staff got excited over every single proposition made to us, so it required Titi and me to determine which ones were real or fake. We were so busy rebuilding our brand that we had little time for foolishness.

A third party, not a distributor but one of those middlemen

who act as coordinators for the big retailers, had written to us saying that Target was holding meetings for potential product companies. They were thinking about creating a new category for their shelves. Since it wasn't Target that was the source of this information, we hit the delete button.

We thought these emails were classic solicitations designed to get our attention. We had neither the time to invest in such foolishness nor the stomach for the disappointment of a bait-and-switch routine. In any event, we had our eyes on other, somewhat smaller partners, like Sephora, Ulta, or perhaps a few upscale department stores—not Target, the mega-chain store with some of the best branding in the business, which had somehow made bargain shopping cool. Why would a mass retailer like Target even want a boutique brand like Miss Jessie's, anyway?

Weeks passed, and a few more emails were ignored, before we got a phone call. It was the third-party company again. This time they spoke to one of our customer service reps, an older Southern woman. She swung in the office that Titi and I shared and announced: "Umm, I got Target on the phone, and they say they want Miss Jessie's! Y'all better get on the phone with them." Of course we took the call. As we were about to push the connect button, Titi said, "It would be funny if this really were Target."

"We have been trying to reach you for some time. Is everything okay? This is a big opportunity for you," the voice on the other end of the phone stated with equal parts concern and enthusiasm. "Target's taking meetings tomorrow, and they want to see you."

We wanted to be sure it wasn't just another sales pitch, so we decided to call his bluff. "Oh yeah, and where is this meeting?"

"Minneapolis."

When we got off the phone, there was a moment of silence. Anybody who knows anything knows Target's headquarters is in Minneapolis. It really was Target after all. In the next moment we made up our minds to change our tone and position on this now important matter. Everyone in the office just stared at us in wide-eyed disbelief. My assistant, who'd seen the initial emails, was especially nervous, clucking around us like a mother hen.

Investigate before you dismiss. Don't assume you know everyone's motives. When you filter too much, you risk overlooking a golden opportunity.

"Is this really happening?" he asked me. "I mean, Target is this huge machine. They don't just invite little companies like ours to come over."

Then it dawned on us. We were standing on the verge of a total game changer.

"Oh my God, oh my God, oh my God!" we screamed. "This *is* real! We need to go!"

Not that we were in any way ready. We had no information or contacts to help us prepare for this whole new world of mass retail. My assistant rushed to put together products and brochures and whatever he could find to make us seem at least halfway knowledgeable. He was on edge the whole day, fussing and fretting. "This is going to be like a giant standing over two little people. Shouldn't you bring a lawyer, at least?" he asked.

"We think we're done with lawyers," we told him. "Besides, there's no time."

"Shouldn't you do some more research?" another employee asked.

We prepared makeshift sales sheets on each product, created an order sheet, and gathered as much information as we could on our brand, including our most impressive press—the *O* double-page spread, *Allure, Essence,* and *Elle* write-ups—and practiced recounting our story of how Miss Jessie's came about and how important our products were in the natural-hair community. We were scrambling and didn't have time to feel anything. We just wanted to get there to see what they were talking about. But we were confident that we knew more about natural hair than any other brand, and we remained equally confident that our products were among the best on the market. That confidence had carried us a long way, and now we needed it to take us all the way to Minneapolis.

Titi and I booked last-minute flights to Target's headquarters for the next day, which cost a fortune. That night I thanked God for putting this opportunity in front of me, and I prayed that no matter the outcome of the meeting, I would have the wisdom to understand it. Just as I drifted off, I realized that I needed to start dreaming a bigger dream for me, my son, and Miss Jessie's.

The next morning, I did not need the alarm clock. I was ready and eager to get on the six-forty-five flight to Minneapolis. Titi and I rode in the cab together, and we strategized what we would say and exactly how we would say it all the way from New York to Minneapolis. We agreed that I would chime in when necessary, but Titi would take the lead. That decision brought me an instant sense of relief. All my life, I had admired my big sister's aptitude for words, her rich deep voice, and her precise diction. Titi spoke with authority and commanded respect in all situations.

When we reached our destination, we were not alone. There were other people—indeed, teams of people—in the waiting area. In contrast to Titi and me, they looked comfortable and seemed at ease. We imagined that their teams consisted of lawyers, accountants, and consultants, and we guessed that their folders and briefcases were stuffed with pie charts, graphs, and sales sheets. We had none of that. We had each other, as always, as well as our products and our nerves.

A pleasant and pretty young blond woman, Carrie North, walked right up to us and said, "Hi, Miss Jessie's, I am so glad you were able to make it!" Carrie was so familiar and friendly, we knew she was trying to put us at ease. But we were starting to feel butterflies in our stomachs while we were waiting for our turn to be seen.

When we finally entered the conference room, the first thing we did was apologize for our lack of preparedness. Other than the small amount of product my assistant had packed for us, we had none of the things people typically present to lobby for product on the shelves. We had no posse of sales representatives. It was just the two of us and our story. Titi and I sat side by side as we always do, grabbing each other's hand under the table before we pressed the "hit it" button.

As Titi began to speak, the attractive head beauty buyer, with a huge diamond on her wedding finger, cut us off. "It's okay, you don't have to tell us your story, we already know Miss Jessie's well. We've seen it in the press, and I always loved your packaging. We just want to place an order. What do you recommend we buy?"

I kicked Titi under the table—my signal for her to switch gears and start selling, for fear of losing this surreal moment.

Titi had paused for a slight second, but I didn't want to risk it. I put my right leg under my butt to give myself more height from my seat and straightened up my posture to tell them they should order EVERYTHING! Titi chimed in when my mouth got dry from talking at jet speed, describing in more detail the difference in each product. At the end of the meeting, they bought most of our product range.

Everyone seemed friendly. The buyer, the diversity person, the distributor, all of the Target representatives in the room. It was different from our last experience with a retailer. They had had a straightforward "our way or the highway" approach. Culturally, this was a different experience from doing business in New York. Many of the people at the table had a singsong accent that used an exclamation point and a question mark at the end of most sentences. They were simply charming. With their blond hair, blue eyes, and apple cheeks, they could have come from central casting for the movie *Fargo*.

It was an emotional moment. In that hotel conference room, I was so overwhelmed that I feared my knees would buckle and I would faint from the extra heat I was feeling in my casual-corporate ensemble: a buttoned-up blue shirt with a black V-neck sweater. But then I pulled it together and asked: "Umm, would it be okay if I took a picture of you guys to catch this moment? This is really big for us."

"Well . . . okay!" they said.

That was it. We'd made it into the big leagues with nothing more than a smile and a handshake. No lawyer, no representative, and no knowledge of mass retail whatsoever. The products that we had made by hand at our kitchen table only a few short years ago would soon be in Target stores across the country.

This event validated the Miss Jessie's brand and our company. With a single meeting, the Miss Jessie's brand and products graduated from an underground curly cult classic to a national brand. The moment every consumer brand yearns for—national recognition and placement on the shelves of a big box store— just fell into our laps.

We assumed this meant more money. It's impossible to over-state the impact a deal like this can have on any small business. It's utterly transformational. Over-night, a brand becomes national, the number of units sold multiply exponentially, and revenues grow from six figures to seven or eight figures.

Don't be surprised by what flies in your window. Good things come to those who persevere, often when they least expect it.

Titi and I celebrated across the street from Target's headquarters with a glass of champagne at Zelo, clinking our glasses together as we made lists of all the people we would call to share the news: our mother, our father, and Uncle Irvin, for starters. We couldn't wait to hear their reactions.

That night I felt particularly close to my sister.

"Miko, we wouldn't be here if it weren't for you," she told me.

Although we had long since reconciled, we never spoke much about the lawsuit. We were running the business and get-ting it done, but we were finally back to being a true sister act. We had been through so much, and I could not help but think that those hard times were meant to prepare us for the success to follow. Now that we were on the national stage, there would be no time for bad blood, hurt feelings, and lawsuits. We were sisters building an empire, and there was no place for division.

As I lay my head down to sleep that night, I also thought of Miss Jessie. For my entire life, I was so very proud to be her granddaughter. That night I felt she had me in her sights, and in that moment I knew she was proud to be my grandmother.

BUILDING YOUR DREAM

★

A Simple Small-Business Recipe

Step One

Find the opportunity. Observe and absorb everything around you to find out what people want and what is missing in the marketplace. Combine this information with your true passion and natural talent to put together the big idea.

Step Two

Set the standard. Source only the best possible ingredients or components to ensure that you are not just the first to market but the best. When the competition catches on, you will keep your customer's loyalty.

Step Three

Leverage the resources you have. Once the concept has been developed and the prototype has been created, start small. If you have to work out of your garage, kitchen, or basement, so be it. If you have a parent, sister, cousin, aunt, or uncle willing to pitch in and offer skills or time for free, even better. You'd be surprised how far you can get without huge piles of capital.

Step Four

Communicate expectations clearly. This applies to any small business that is a partnership. Whether you are in business with a family member, friend, or associate, establish in writing exactly who does what and who has ultimate control. Leave no room for ambiguity.

Step Five

Use grassroots networks to get the word out. Let your brand's reputation build by word of mouth. Use social media and start building personal relationships with smaller vendors who will carry your product. Invest in some PR.

Step Six

Pace yourself. Be careful not to expand too much, too fast. Many small businesses die because they get too cocky about their growth prospects and overleveraged.

Step Seven

Find a mentor. Find someone in your field or industry whom you admire, and reach out. Many more seasoned and successful entrepreneurs are looking to pay it forward and flattered to be tapped for their expertise. Try to do this early on in your career, then proceed with caution. As you become more established, not everyone who approaches you will have altruistic motives. These relationships can be mutually beneficial as long as you first figure out where they are coming from and what, if anything, they want from you.

Step Eight

Keep the cash! While it may be tempting to pay and treat yourself once you start seeing some sustained sales, resist. What you don't reinvest in the business or an asset such as real estate, put into a savings account. Stay debt-free and build a safety cushion. Maintaining liquidity will protect you from the unforeseen, such as a lost customer, unexpected litigation, or a general economic downturn.

Step Nine

Prepare for growth. You will reach a point where you can't do everything by yourself. As your business takes off, you may need to outsource distribution and manufacturing. You may also need a larger space or warehouse. Take steps to ensure that when the next big order comes, you will have the capacity. Continue to manage growth by adapting operations and adding resources accordingly.

Step Ten

Hire wisely. When you are launching a new business, you don't need a lot of hands on deck, but you do need at least one or two trusted employees. Interview carefully, and don't just consider how the candidate comes across on paper. You want like-minded people who are willing to pitch in and do whatever needs to be done, regardless of job description and title.

Step Eleven

Blow it up. Keep communicating with your customers about the latest product or company news. Get creative, and go beyond your industry's trade shows to festivals, concerts, anywhere your customer might be. Interact with these consumers, hand out free samples, do demos. Let them know that you are the face of the brand and create that personal connection. These moves will get you talked about where it counts.

Step Twelve

Evolve your product line. Once you've established your brand, keep it moving with new categories, more options, and a healthy range of choices. Don't launch a product just because everyone else is doing it. Pay close attention to customer feedback on social media or, as in our case, through salons and retail, to find out how your customer's tastes and needs are changing. When she expresses a desire, it's your opportunity to meet that through brand extension.

Step Thirteen

Pick a partner, or don't. As your company grows and you get on the radar of bigger players, there's going to come a time when you get invited to the big leagues. This is good news; it's the outcome that so many small-business owners dream of. But don't leap blindly at the first offer.

Consider what you'll be giving up (autonomy and ownership) as well as what you'll gain (money, access, scale). If
the offer requires you to give up too much of the identity the brand has been built on, it may not be worth it.
Never be afraid to sit out a dance or two.

★ ★ ★

Twelve

NEW GROWTH

Competition is the keen cutting edge of business.

—HENRY FORD

When we struck the Target deal, we were on a high. We shared what we knew of the deal with our family. We also spoke with a small handful of individuals we trusted with a few details of our business, and they filled in many of the blanks of what the Target deal meant. Thank God we'd outsourced our distribution less than a month earlier. We had no idea of the full value that outsourcing would bring us with this new mass account. Luckily, we had worked out the kinks in the new system just in time for the avalanche of orders about to hit us. Without that, we would not have had the capacity to leverage the huge opportunity.

Because we were not prepared, it seemed like the big-box relationship brought with it new rules. It was a whole new phase of growth that required us to adapt—and fast. Reaching that level in retail isn't the end of your problems, it's the beginning of a whole new set of complications, and the learning curve is high. We were a small company, unschooled in the ways of mass retail. We didn't know the lingo, and we didn't have any contacts or anyone we could talk to about it. Worse, we didn't realize how extensive the gaps in our retail knowledge really were.

There was no time to waste as we familiarized ourselves with terms like "planograms" (store layout for product placement), "SKUs" (stock keeping units), and "ad dollars" (when an advertisement is camera-ready). There's a big difference between learning words and learning a language, understanding what these words mean, and knowing that they have consequences. That first year, we were being asked to deliver and be responsive to all kinds of things, and half the time we had no idea what they were asking for. But what a problem to have!

To try to get a handle on it, I viewed it like a first date at the big dance. It felt like love at first sight, but I quickly understood that, as partners, we really did not know each other very well. What we did know about one another, we liked, but we needed to get to know more. From my perspective, the Miss Jessie's team was like the girl from the other side of town (or maybe even the wrong side of the tracks), and the Target team was like "big man on campus" that everybody adored. We had never been invited to this sort of party before and everything was new. Compared with Target's other "partners," I am sure that we were a little rough around the edges, unsophisticated, and certainly less familiar with the rules involved when "courting" Target. Our first few "dances" with Target were a bit rough and clumsy. To be sure, we stepped on each other's toes and made some mistakes. But over time, we found our rhythm and were dancing in step. Target showed us a few new moves; some we loved and some we didn't, and so we had to make adjustments. We also taught Target some new steps as well as showing the firm that for this relationship to work, we would not be spun around the floor like some others: we needed to move together and at a pace that made sense to us. In the end, Target was a willing partner and understood that we added something new and exciting to the overall dance. We earned mutual respect. Before long, Target was inviting more and more partners to join. At times the dance floor feels a bit overcrowded with new partners coming and going, but that's part of the experience and it keeps everyone on their toes. I learned the dance pretty quickly, learned how to keep up, and even invented a few new steps, because I was certain that I was not going to lose my partner.

As we familiarized ourselves with a whole new level of the retail industry, in many ways we were also changing the way things were done. Almost from the beginning, we understood that the Miss Jessie's mission was bigger than catering to black women. Because we were working in the salon and serviced an ethnically diverse group of women, we knew that there was a world of curly-haired women—not just black

The most successful business owners know they must continually evolve and learn if they want to play in the big leagues.

women with curly hair. That is a big and important distinction. Our philosophy was to address the texture of the hair and not the color of the skin. Honestly, our approach was no different from other beauty brands that address a particular beauty need. For example, body moisturizers are aimed at women with dry skin, oily skin, or perhaps sensitive skin—but you would never promote a product as exclusively for women with dark skin or white skin. It would be offensive. It is the condition of the skin that matters, not the color of the skin. Yet for reasons that I still do not completely understand, the hair sections in most major retail chain stores are completely segregated by race and have nothing to do with hair texture.

Initially, there was absolute resistance from retail partners to placing the Miss Jessie's products anywhere other than in the ethnic sections of their stores. There was even an unwillingness to place the Miss Jessie's products in the "pro" or "salon" hair-care products sections—even though I had been a stylist for over two decades and the Miss Jessie's products were first widely distributed through salons. Apparently, because we were black and the majority of our customers were black, the products had to be placed in the ethnic section, even though women of every color with curly hair knew about, used, and would buy the products.

Placing our products in the ethnic section had no appeal to us because the beauty aesthetic, price point, and brand origins of most products found in the ethnic section were in conflict with the Miss Jessie's products and philosophy. Big-box retailers carried ethnic hair products that mostly centered on relaxer hair care, which caters to straight styling. In contrast, the Miss Jessie's products are all about celebrating and caring for wavy, curly, and kinky hair and offer a completely different beauty aesthetic. In the store aisle, you typically saw greases, hair oils, and other random on-off products, which were manufactured and marketed by companies that could have just as easily made any other commodity, with prices ranging from two dollars for a single item to seven dollars for a set that included a whole relaxer kit. Placing these products right next to the Miss Jessie's premium-priced, salon-inspired products made little sense. Typically, products in the ethnic section sat cramped on the bottom of the shelf, badly lit, poorly packaged, and gathering dust. They weren't much of a moneymaker for the retailer, and they didn't offer much choice to the consumer. The retailers viewed the customer who bought this product as someone who wouldn't build a big enough shopping basket, so they seemingly didn't care about her or her needs.

Target was among the leaders to recognize that a change was needed. Target introduced the retail chain shoppers to a new "multicultural" and "textured" hair section that came closest to the Miss Jessie's philosophy of addressing hair texture rather than skin color. To its credit, Target went all out and secured end-cap placement for its assortment of hair-care products designed for curly hair. In the chain-store retail world, end-cap placement is highly coveted, because end caps showcase certain products and are intended to attract the shopper's attention without the need to walk into the aisle. It is a subtle but significant statement and a testament to Target's true commitment to speaking to and respecting all of its guests, and this made Target an attractive partner.

Likewise, from our brownstone in Brooklyn, Miss Jessie's

was making a lot of noise. We were switching the hair images of Eurocentric beauty to highly textured hair on beautiful women of many ethnicities, mainly African-Americans who used to buy relaxer kits. We also put a spotlight on the white and Latina women whose curls we were doing in Bedford-Stuyvesant. By the time we reached Target, our product had been on the market for five years. Paired up with our images were the how-tos, which we shared in the universe free of charge. This knockout combination directly affected the ethnic aisles in mass retail, as well as the beauty salon.

Over time, the Miss Jessie's philosophy of addressing hair texture without regard to race gained more appreciation and acceptance. Presently, almost all retailers are renaming or have already renamed their "ethnic" hair-care section. Indeed, it is more common to see "multicultural," "textured," "natural," or simply "curly" hair sections, which are now spruced up and designed to entice guests. We take pride in having played a role in this necessary evolution. Now, whether Miss Jessie's products are placed on end caps or in line, it makes sense that the category of products is speaking to texture.

STROLLING THE AISLES

★

Putting together that deal with Target was such a whirlwind, it didn't even seem real. One cold weeknight evening in March 2010, we decided we had to see the store display for ourselves.

"Let's go check out the Target on Atlantic Avenue," I told my sister as we were getting ready to leave the office.

We had a full display facing the larger aisles where most of the customer traffic walked through the store, or what is known in the industry as an "end cap," with attractive images and ad copy surrounding our jars and tubes of hair product. We couldn't wait to see it. But when we walked into the Brooklyn location, the first thing we noticed was that there was hardly any product on the shelf—it had sold out so fast. Titi and I rearranged our section, displaying the jars so they popped, and had started taking pictures of ourselves when a couple of customers recognized us. We conversed with them, offering hair tips. Soon the aisle was filled with women asking for product prescriptions and advice. It was almost as if we'd set up an impromptu hair clinic right by our end cap.

Experiencing the customers' reception was confirmation that our presence in Target would be a shot in the arm for an otherwise lifeless category. Sales in the ethnic aisle for relaxers were down about 30 percent at the large retailers. Target wanted to change all of that and had gotten wise to the fact that this lost customer was spending up to fifty-eight dollars for a jar of Baby Buttercreme. "Who knew?" one of its merchandisers exclaimed, thrilled by the dramatic turnaround.

Now this customer was on the mass retailer's radar in a huge way. Target began to understand that she was willing to make an investment and spend on things that mattered to her. With companies like Miss Jessie's demonstrating that this customer had money to spend, Target was taking every step to get her to walk through its doors and linger, with better lighting, more creative displays, and greater prominence in the store aisle.

GOOD, BETTER, BEST

★

We were excited to have caught Target's attention and to have earned our end-cap placement in stores. Because I tend to stay focused on my own business and have no control over what my competitors do, I am rarely concerned with them. I assumed that when dealing with Target, I would continue to focus on my own business. That changed a bit. I quickly came to appreciate that from time to time Target (like most other retailers) was more interested in maintaining and managing the entire category of products rather than focusing on a particular, individual brand. For the first time, I had to give serious thought to the entire category of natural hair and curly hair–care products, which meant evaluating competitors and understanding competition. It was critical for me to understand Miss Jessie's value proposition to the entire caterory and leverage that value. What made Miss Jessie's necessary to the mix? If I could not answer that simple question, then there was a problem. Shelf space is limited and costly, and if a brand cannot earn its keep, then it's off the shelf and out of the store. Ultimately, I reached the conclusion that every brand in the category— just like Miss Jessie's—had a function and played a particular role. Target wanted to offer its guests variety. Hence, the good, the better, and the best model. Miss Jessie's role was the high-performing, salon-inspired, and premium-priced original hair-care product for natural and curly hair. No other brand, then or now, can legitimately make that claim or play that role. As important as Target was to Miss Jessie's, I understood that Miss Jessie's was important to Target as well. Including Miss

Jessie's in the selection added credibility to the category in a way that no other brand could do.

Before we came along, the mass retailer's highest-priced hair product in the ethnic aisle was around $5.95, and an "expensive" item in this category was unheard of. Mass retailers did not believe that a customer would care about her hair to the point where she was willing to spend whatever it took for the desired results. Before Miss Jessie's proved that customer base was powerful, it would have been difficult for a brand and product to command a sticker price of higher than seven dollars. Shoppers were not hesitating to pay thirty-eight dollars for a professional-sized jar of Curly Pudding or fifty-eight dollars for a jar of Baby Buttercreme. This proved that our pricing could work, creating a middle ground for other brands to come in under our price. Miss Jessie's proved the unthinkable, making a place for competing brands to come to market and charge nineteen dollars or even twenty-five and still be considered reasonably priced compared with an item from the Miss Jessie's product line. All in all, the category was elevated, creating a vessel for other independent and often minority- or women-owned grassroots start-up businesses to set up shop en masse.

As good as our presence in Target was for other brands, the move was good for us, too, for obvious reasons. We could generate significantly higher sales volume and gain nationwide brand recognition. We could not have paid for this kind of marketing. We have to give Target credit for giving Miss Jessie's a premium spot.

When the news hit that we were going in Target stores, "the industry," including competitors, our existing salon partners/retailers, and suppliers, were quick to say we would fail.

"You know they are going to slash their prices," one of them said.

"You know you just sold your soul to the devil," said another.

"Don't come running back to us when they destroy your business," our smaller mom-and-pop shops said.

"You will never be able to keep your price point in Target," a distributor told us.

"Just who do they think they are, going into Target without cutting their prices?" asked a customer on Facebook, one of many who hoped to get their favorite Miss Jessie's product for less.

"They should go to Sephora or Ulta, not Target. That's crazy!" commented several beauty bloggers.

Before Target contacted us, we had always envisioned our product in Sephora. We even sent them our product range after researching submissions guidelines online. We got rejected. But Target had the vision. Some of our competitors laughed and told us we were making a dumb move, as they vowed to stay out of mass. At a trade show, one of them even told us, "We don't play those mass games."

We proved everyone wrong. Initially, most of our sales had been through our website, and Internet consumers don't usually distinguish between whether a brand is found in Sephora, CVS, or Target. That meant we didn't need to be too precious about who carried our product as long as they were doing right by us in terms of promotion and product placement. The key to our next phase of growth was to make the product as widely available as possible, and that's what being in Target did for us; customers were excited to get it at their neighborhood Target.

The partnership has been a huge success. We've gone from being in 225 Target stores in 2010 to being in nearly every Target store. Target has been happy with our sales, and we've been a permanent fixture on the end caps—something that's unheard of in the retail industry. And this approach is winning.

LEARNING CURVE

★

As in all new relationships, we hit a few bumps—big ones. When you are pioneering a new product category, this is bound to happen. In a sense, we were all feeling our way through unfamiliar territory.

Early on, a few of our retailers, including mass, did what they would do with any of the other brands they carried—they reduced prices. The problem was, they had promised they would not. Word came to us quickly, through one of our disgruntled retail partners in Atlanta—a smaller player who was justifiably angry over being undercut by a retail giant. It was not something that we had agreed to, and we were not happy.

Pricing has always been a big issue with our big-box retail partners, who initially did not understand or appreciate our marketing strategy. We wanted our promotions to be an event and meaningful. Prior to entering big-box chain stores, we had a traditional Buy One Get One (the "BOGO") Free promotion. It was Titi's idea. This promotion became our way of spreading brand awareness, because it allowed people to try the products. We also wanted to show our appreciation to our loyal Miss Jessie's fans, and it is our way of giving back. That's one of the reasons why we plan the BOGO at Christmas time and toward the end of the year when folks are more likely to spend on affordable luxuries. As a child, I remember how much everyone around me wanted Christmas to be special, and it makes me happy to think that the Miss Jessie's products will be a part of someone's holiday. The BOGO offer is very expensive for the business, but we always plan ahead for it, because it has become a Miss Jessie's tradition. We explained our marketing approach to our retail partners, who at first agreed but then later reneged. When our first big-box partner started to discount the products, it turned our marketing strategy upside down and created instant chaos. It was their product now, and they could do with it what they wanted. I understood that. But what if they did not have the product or could not get the product? If we stopped shipping the product, then at least one problem would be solved. But other problems would follow.

Though we understood the stakes, we felt it was critical to stick to our principles. Despite what we might lose, we weighed our options and stayed focused on what we *did* have. We knew we could afford to say no to mass retail because we were already profitable and ran our business and personal finances with surgical efficiency. We asked ourselves if we were happy with what we had on our own, which was more than we'd ever dreamed. The answer was yes, we were willing to risk a whole lot of money—more than we had ever seen from one account. When we opened our first banking statement after the first few checks were deposited, we were in disbelief.

As we tried to salvage the situation with the retailer, raising our objections, they appeared unconcerned. Indeed, even our own marketing liaison with mass, warned us that if we complained too much, we'd lose the account. In the end, we had to take that chance.

"Okay, stop shipments," I told everyone.

"What? You can't do that!" shrieked our bookkeeper. "You risk losing the whole account."

Our whole team, including Titi, was looking at me as if I had two heads. We had to stick to the marketing strategy that we knew worked. I held firm, well aware of what it could mean for the relationship. Once she understood my reasoning, Titi was on board with the decision.

It was a costly lesson all around. We left a few million dollars on the table, and the brief absence of our products from the shelf allowed our competitors to gain momentum. Reporting data companies IRI and Nielsen, which the industry relies on to report sales, were tracking our competitors' robust growth while we were showing zilch.

Be true to yourself, no matter who you are doing business with. Never forget the core values and authentic style that brought you success in the first place.

After some back-and-forth with the big-box retailer, we reached an agreement with our partner. It was a good lesson, reminding us that as we scaled up, we had to stay hypervigilant about what was happening in these stores, in order to maintain consistency and stick to our core principles as a business.

A NEW PLAYBOOK

★

It would have been all too easy to become complacent and go by everyone else's playbook. The money was flowing in, so who were we to question the conventional wisdom? The mass retail industry has a set of rules and certain ways of doing business, but those rules just did not make full sense for our business. We did not understand, for example, why we had to pay a distributor an extra 15 to 25 percent more of our business when retailers like Target, CVS, Walmart, or Walgreens came directly to us. We already had a fulfillment company and shipper and did not need those additional services. We did not understand why we would be charged for damages that could not be confirmed. We were confused as to why we had to pay advertising allowances that would not guarantee we would even appear in the retailer's ads or circulars. There was a long list of additional charges and deductions for the privilege of doing business with mass retail, and we dared to question all of these practices. But we weren't presenting all of these challenges just to be difficult. We simply did not have the extra money to throw away on unjustifiable expenses. Our mass partner's power was undeniable, but so was our desire for autonomy. We have learned to forge a balance between the two.

> *Be bold. It is always possible to rewrite the rules if you dare to ask.*

DECISIONS, DECISIONS

★

As we made the news, consultants and middlemen were coming out of the woodwork, making promises and offering solutions that seemed self-serving and unethical. Some came highly recommended by our retail partners. When you enter into these big-box deals, there's an entire industry of marketing people, distributors, brokers, manufacturing subcontractors, and private investors who want a piece of the action, promising to make your life easier as they show you the ropes.

My discerning nature runs high and deep on a normal daily basis, so I was experiencing extra paranoia as we entered this early engagement with mass retail. Years earlier, we had been running a top-secret business from our home, and we kept that self-protective mind-set when it came to growing our business. It took time to feel fully confident and trust in the process, or at least it did for me. Titi was a little more prepared to dive right in. She wanted Miss Jessie's to reach its highest heights and was pushing for growth. She thought it wise to shake some of the old, super-secretive ways in which we did business. She encouraged me to put fear aside and listen to some of the things these people wanted to share with us. "Hell," she said, "it might be to our benefit." Titi imagined that at this high level of corporate and mass retail

Don't be afraid to make your own decisions. When something doesn't pass the smell test, it's for a reason.

business, individuals would be cooler and more laid-back in their willingness to help and share information. She made a convincing case, so I set aside my suspicions and gave the new relationships a try.

One new relationship came referred by a buyer from our retail partner. This person introduced us to the owners of a company that was not in the hair space at the time but had some experience in mass retail with other products and was hoping to get into the hair category. It was perplexing to me that this kind of connection was being heavily pushed. After they launched their hair line, they would become a direct competitor. However, the buyer insisted that this company could help us grow our mom-and-pop business and that we should speak with them.

We all met and went to dinner. Titi and I personally liked the principals of this company. We even formed a kind of family bond. Later on, when they gave us a tour of their facility, we were able to see their hustle. It looked a lot like our operation, and I was particularly proud to see their accomplishments. I wasn't sure how they planned to make it in the natural-hair-care category, moving from their core business, but I wished them the best.

Our new friends offered to make our products for us. They also offered to ship to our mass retailer, explaining that they wanted to ensure we get on board as smoothly as possible. As we processed the proposition, my paranoia and fear kicked in. Doing business together in this way would have required us to turn over our product formulas—the very things we had invested so much time and trouble to develop and protect. It was like asking Colonel Sanders to hand over his secret recipe. They could have knocked off our product with that information. In the arrangement, they would have been privy to all kinds of other proprietary information, including how much product we were shipping and how much money we were making.

I've never pretended to be a sophisticated businesswoman. Once things start getting fancy, I admit I can get lost. In this case, it prohibited me from speaking my lack of understanding out loud. Maybe, I thought, this was a normal way of doing business in mass retail. Maybe I was missing something. At one point, our new friends said, "This ain't no nigger shit!"

Their unfortunate choice of words aside, perhaps they were right. Perhaps I needed to adjust my way of doing business and go with their suggested strategy. It left me feeling conflicted. Most of all, I did not want to let Titi down. I had promised her I would be more open to new concepts as we ventured into this uncharted territory. Luckily, Titi took the pressure off. Realizing the concerns, she was not confident about what the partnership offered. Although we remained on good terms with our new friends and we greatly respect them, we turned down the offer.

MISSING A MENTOR

★

The more recognized we became in the industry, the more people wanted something from us, and those relationships weren't always in our best interests. One gentleman in particular, who was known to us as someone in the urban community with tremendous brand expertise and a track record of success, approached us and offered to take us under his wing.

We were thrilled to meet with this man in his office and spend time with him. He told us he would protect us and never let anyone take advantage of us—not our competitors, not our mass retailers, not even our men. Titi and I had long been hoping to meet a mentor, and we were dazzled by his ideas and insights. But I was having a hard time understanding the value of his proposition. "What do you want in exchange?" I asked.

Know who you are dealing with, and what they may want from you. The higher you go and the more money you make, the more you may encounter shark-infested waters.

It quickly became clear that he wanted ownership in Miss Jessie's. After one more meeting, we were sure we were not interested in having a partner. Many more investors started approaching us, but we could see through their pitches, which were misleading at best. We began to wonder if there was anyone out there we could trust.

We wanted guidance as we navigated the foreign waters of big business. We really needed someone to sit down, talk with us, and school us. We wanted a well-known person in the community to coach us. True mentors were missing. Those first two years of our relationship with mass retailers, our lean team of fewer than ten employees, including Titi and me, ended up having to do it all. The outside people who were supposed to help us were a consistent disappointment, from the liaison company we asked to track inventory and sales to those competitors posing as allies. By doing it all ourselves, we could learn the industry, figure out what worked for us, and discard the approaches that did not fit with our core values as a business.

I wasn't afraid to stand up for myself. Collectively, our recent experiences had made us stronger and more seasoned as businesswomen. As my beloved uncle Irvin told me, "You were dragged through the mud with your white suit on, and you still didn't get dirty!" When the so-called experts advised us to acquiesce to the big-box retailers' demands, we decided to challenge the standard way of doing business by cutting out the middlemen, handling our own mass retail distribution, and dealing with our mass retail partner directly.

You know your own business better than most experts do.

ATTENTION TO DETAIL

★

Our current relationship with these retailers is unique, with a more open line of communication, which enhances our efficiency. We've been instrumental in advising them and helping them create a whole new market, lending them authenticity and credibility with our grassroots Brooklyn story and background.

One thing that distinguishes our relationships with these partners is the level of control we are given. We are just as selective when choosing locations to present our products in larger retail stores as we were when considering which smaller retail and beauty supply stores to go with. What we have learned over the years is that not all stores are created equal in terms of where we can get the best sales volume and traffic. At first we thought we needed to be in as many stores as possible. But in mass retail, there is something called the 80/20 rule, meaning about 20 percent of stores do about 80 percent of the business. This is particularly true for some of our products that cater to more coily/kinky hair types. It makes sense, for example, to carry a more diverse range in Washington, D.C., than, say, Madison, Wisconsin.

As we have taken our time to drill down and learn this business, we've adjusted our strategy accordingly. Now we select which products go where, according to the demographic of the store location. Most of the stores carry our current top sellers—Pillow Soft, Leave In Condish, Jelly Soft Curls, Multicultural Curls, and Quick Curls—because these products can be used on any curl type, regardless of ethnicity. Product development is a constant at Miss Jessie's. We never stand still.

Thirteen

★ ★ ★

BIG ROLLERS

Ain't no stoppin' us now.

—McFADDEN & WHITEHEAD

It was a rare night out, away from business, for me in May 2013. *Black Enterprise* magazine was holding an event at Jay-Z's 40/40 Club in New York City—the Good Life Reception—to kick off their program for entrepreneurs. The party was full of media, entertainment, and industry folk mixing it up. Miss Jessie's was sponsoring that night with gift bags, and Titi was out with friends. Instead of my usual sidekick, I brought along my legal counsel, whose company and witty banter I had come to enjoy.

When we arrived, the place was packed. We found an empty bank of couches, took a seat, and observed the crowd.

Almost instantly, that spot turned into a natural-hair-care hub, with bloggers, stylists, product owners, and even some of my natural-hair clients. The music was pumping, the conversation was flying, and all around us, people were air-kissing and hugging. A woman sat down on the one empty seat next to me. When I turned to my right to see who it was, she was facing me. "Hello, Miko," she said in a manner that was plain and pleasant.

At first I was taken aback by her beauty and did not recognize her. She had a deep, rich chocolate complexion, with pretty, big brown eyes, a gorgeous smile, and a wonderfully big Pony Puff. It was Karen Tappin-Saunderson, the owner of Karen's Body Beautiful, a line of hair and beauty products.

"I just wanted to thank you and your sister for what you have done in this industry for brands like mine," she told me. "You know, I built my grassroots business in Brooklyn, too, and if it weren't for you being the trailblazer, it may not have been possible for my company to be in Target."

Never tear down your competition. If you are confident in your product, you can afford to be magnanimous.

I was at a loss for words, preoccupied with trying to hold back my tears. All these years of grinding in our brownstone, we'd thought we were alone on this journey. We had no idea that we were making a difference in the lives of so many other entrepreneurs who, in many ways, were just like Karen. It was nice to know that our hard work was not going unnoticed.

That night Karen revealed to me that her business was now focused on hair. Many businesses both big and small had made some adjustments to their product lines, shifting to natural and curly hair after seeing what a profitable business it had become.

KEEP IT COMING

★

It was a timely reminder that Titi and I needed to push ahead and keep carving our own path. Maintaining success as an entrepreneur requires constant reinvention. The competition was great motivation for Titi and me to continue pioneering through product innovation and creative marketing strategies. This period was about managing our growth in the right way, evolving our strategy according to the current market realities, while never losing sight of who we were at our core. Miss Jessie's was a brand with integrity, and we aimed to keep it that way.

But maintaining our identity did not preclude change. We had to develop new products and business strategies, reconfigure our operations, find new partners, upgrade our salon services, and adjust our marketing and promotions to stay ahead of the game. Like Miss Jessie always told us, only a fool takes success for granted. We had no business being complacent.

It was especially important to get out in front of everybody else in terms of product innovation. Sales of all the products in our range have been robust for all our retail partners, since we offer our customers an increasing array of options that responds directly to her needs.

Keep it moving. No business can afford to rest on past success.

We started out as a salon-focused product in 2004, when

we first came out with Curly Pudding. We were a boutique brand. But although we will always take inspiration from our salon clients, our customer's needs have changed. She's done the Big Chop, and she's more educated about her own naturally curly hair. She doesn't necessarily need Curly Pudding to define and show every single curl on her head. We created that rich, decadent product for her because there was something to prove—that she had workable, natural-hair texture with a curl pattern. But now that she has a head of grown-out, gorgeous, healthy hair, the aesthetic has changed. She wants a wash-and-go option. She is more comfortable experimenting and may want something softer, with less hold. We've developed a number of new products to support this style—like Pillow Soft, Jelly Soft, Multicultural Curls, Transitioner's Magic, or Leave In Condish.

We've made a number of adjustments within the line, including some changes for the mass market. There is a more relaxed attitude to curl now, so we can cater to customers who don't need the rich and decadent consistency of Curly Pudding. Some of these new products are the direct result of the dialogue we have with our customers. My dear friend Emma, for example, told me she wanted a wash-and-go look that was more like an Afro, with a little control and definition to the curl and without the firm hold. She's come a long way from those early days when she didn't want to chop off her straightened hair, as have so many of our clients and customers.

Be a work in progress. The most successful business owners know they must continually evolve.

A BIGGER WORLD

★

Our newly launched Coily Custard—a wash-n-go styler to help transform tight and frizzy 'fros into moisturized curls—appeals to this customer. The product was one of three new items we rolled out on Valentine's Day 2014. We'd never unveiled three new products simultaneously. Three is a lot for any brand, but we wanted to make a splash. Besides Coily Custard, we brought out Transitioner's Magic, to help women grow out their processed hair and avoid the Big Chop, and Multicultural Curls.

Multicultural Curls has been one of our most dramatic

Broaden your customer base
by doing the following:

1. Pay close attention to your evolving customer demographics.
2. Take note of who is selecting your product.
3. Don't be surprised if these shoppers are more diverse than you originally believed.
4. Scrutinize the sales reports in each region.
5. You can operate locally, but think globally, because there could be millions of potential new customers far beyond your original footprint.

success stories since we first launched Curly Pudding, and it speaks directly to the changing times. It was partly a tribute to our own biracial heritage—a wink to our mom and dad. Although we started out by focusing on the tighter-coiled texture, we felt it was time to be more inclusive. As mixed-race women, we had experience with many different hair and curl types. Multicultural doesn't necessarily mean biracial, and curl type doesn't always depend on skin tone. It was simply a way of serving a broader customer base.

We live in a global marketplace. Travel to any country and you will see that populations have become melting pots. Very few people are all Russian or all African. Europe is full of curly girls, and Latin and South American women have incredible curl and texture variations. Developing a multicultural product opens us up to the rest of the world. It was simply a smart decision to make in our changing global economy.

It was also validation for the mass retailers, which recently renamed their "ethnic" aisles "multicultural." This was a victory for all of us. For years, retailers used to try to relegate us to the ethnic section, but we were a professional brand that was not just for black women; ours was for all women with curly hair. Our resistance had an impact on how much we could expand. We eventually gave in, realizing that it was better to get our product on the shelf so our customer could have access. But the retailers came around to our way of thinking with the aisle makeover. Being able to partner with retailers as we catered to the broader segment is also why Multicultural Curls is now one of our best-selling products.

MASTER MARKETERS

★

Authenticity has always been the key to our marketing success. You can always hire someone to say anything, but if they really do not mean it, it tends to show. We are proud of the fact that we have included our actual salon clients as models to showcase our salon work and product. An important message behind the Miss Jessie's brand is that natural hair and natural women are beautiful. There is no better way to make that statement than by showcasing real women, who are real clients and real users of the Miss Jessie's products. Titi and I have also been the face of the brand for certain campaigns, in large part because we were the cheapest models that we knew—no modeling fees. We also wanted to have a relationship with the public in general and Miss Jessie's fans in particular. It is odd, but some women use beauty products without ever knowing who makes the products. It is important to me that women understand and know that there are real people behind Miss Jessie's, who actually use the products. We are the faces of the brand because we support and believe in the Miss Jessie's products.

Social media has gained momentum over the last decade and it is another wonderful way for us to connect with our customer. We've found authentic Miss Jessie's lovers and fans via social media and we include them in our ads as well. This approach keeps the message clear that real people use Miss Jessie's. We have even included bloggers in our campaigns, but only if the blogger was a fan of the product first. It is unfortunate, but within the past few years, certain brands have come under attack for paying bloggers for positive reviews or to host events without disclosing to the public that they're being paid and are not a user of the promoted product. We have been lucky enough to have a host of gorgeous bloggers and Miss Jessie's fans who are happy to show their support.

We connected with a wholesome multicultural family in California via Instagram while we were about to launch Multicultural Curls. A mother, father, son, and daughter are captured during a family moment in a Miss Jessie's ad. The father is combing his daughter's hair with the mother and son on the scene. This ad is the most talked-about in the history of Miss Jessie's, because it is relatable, capturing the genuine love of family.

STYLING AHEAD

★

While we never forget our core customer, many of these new products will have a more universal appeal, in terms of both performance and price—one of many things we are doing to target a wider demographic and stay ahead of the competition. In fact, we are finding that many customers who decided to experiment with the "me too" brands have come back to us. There's been a kind of shakeout, with many of the imitators that were trying to grab our market share now disappearing from the shelves.

Michelle Breyer, our friend and the woman at the helm of NaturallyCurly.com, says Miss Jessie's stays on top of it because we "keep people excited" about what we are doing. Every time we come out with something new, our customer knows it's not just to push our brand. We put something out when we see a need for it, and not before.

"You know, with each new product launch, Miss Jessie's keeps reminding people that you've been doing this for a long time," Michelle recently told me. "That Miss Jessie's expertise of yours just cuts through the noise."

UPGRADE

★

Our salon remains a big part of who we are as a brand. As we've matured as a business, we've moved out of our brownstone and into a different, spacious location in the heart of Manhattan's SoHo. We kept that old-world look of decorative moldings, crystal chandeliers, high ceilings, and wood floors, but freshened up in white, with a few accents in the colors of our Miss Jessie's packaging. We call it "comfortable elegance." We have a product store out front, as you enter, and, discreetly hidden in the back, a much larger salon space that runs with clocklike precision. Our grand opening was a big party, full of friends, family, loyal customers, and supporters in social and traditional media—a way of saying thank you for believing in us. Even A'Lelia Bundles, the great-great-granddaughter of Madam C. J. Walker—a major inspiration for our business model—honored us with her presence.

Of course, we didn't change what was working before the move. We have continued our tradition of making our salon clients feel at home with drinks and snacks, and gospel and soul music playing through the speakers. The Miss Jessie's salon is still a destination, where our clients know us and each other. I still come in every Saturday morning and do the hair of our regulars. During the week, the salon remains open, staffed by stylists personally trained and supervised by me. Through that space, I will always be accessible to the naturally curly women who have, through their loyalty and honest feedback, helped us to build this brand. While the location of the salon has changed and may change again, I am confident that the quality of service will not.

TABLE OF TRUTH

★

Down the block on Broadway, where we located our corporate headquarters, the Miss Jessie's team continues along this personal and professional growth track. We routinely talk out our decisions at what we call our "Table of Truth." When one of us has an idea, we ask the others to punch as many holes in it as they can. There is no ego. Everyone carries the weight and takes full responsibility. We share all of our ideas and take ownership as a team, with no one blaming the others if it fails or taking all the credit if it succeeds.

We've never bothered hiring "executives." We don't need a CEO or senior vice president to sit on a high chair and tell people what to do. Titles have no relevance to us. We need smart people who are willing to learn and get their hands dirty with the rest of us. When it comes to the work, we view ourselves as employees. We're standing there alongside everyone else, filling up sample bags for an event, packing, unpacking, and lifting incoming product boxes—whatever it takes.

Our small team battles it out every day, throwing out ideas, challenging them, and making them better. The other team members' perspectives help to keep us on the right path because, although they love the brand, they are not as emotionally attached to it as Titi and me. They weren't in that brownstone all those years with us, and their emotional distance brings objectivity to the choices we now make.

> *Challenge your own beliefs every day. Inviting the honest opinion of your team members and putting your ideas through the fire will make them better.*

MANAGING GROWTH

★

After securing the Target deal, we used the following couple of years as a testing phase. We wanted to understand the enterprise from top to bottom before we made our next move. During that time, we came to understand that there is a price to being in mass retail. Our overheads increased because we had larger orders to fill. We had to hire more staff. Our shipping costs also increased. There were costs that couldn't be measured in dollars and cents, such as missing out on personal time with family, friends, and lovers. We asked ourselves if we had the capacity to make these sacrifices while establishing a plan that would help us manage the business growth and its accompanying personal challenges.

Even though we were dealing with huge corporations, we

had to continue to trust that our own instincts were right for our brand, whatever the industry norms.

POISED FOR GROWTH

★

Eventually, these big players came to realize that what worked for us brought success for them. It is necessary to be open and willing to learn. At the same time, be prepared to go in and fight your ground to establish key terms essential to survive in the mass retail landscape. The big retailers and distributors have plenty of other accounts to worry about, so they're not going to sweat the details like a small business, where one wrong decision can have a devastating impact on the bottom line.

With each new deal, the Miss Jessie's team is growing in confidence, knowledge, and capacity. We are laying the foundation to sell our products internationally, having spent months educating ourselves on the stringent requirements for ingredients used in any product sold within the European Union. We already have customers all over the world, but an official presence would reach more multicultural women who desire hair solutions. The potential for Miss Jessie's is limitless in a diverse world where standards of beauty are changing and women across cultures are freeing themselves from the old norms and embracing their God-given curls.

Miss Jessie's remains lean, nimble, hungry, and entrepreneurial in spirit. Our first foray into the international market is approaching: we are planning a partnership with Boots in the United Kingdom. As negotiations with all kinds of new partners continue, from distributors to national chains, to partners in brand-new markets all over the world, we have never been in a better position to set our own terms as we keep proving the business model we've established with our initial large mass partner.

Financially, and in terms of our current infrastructure, we are poised for growth. For many small businesses, a sudden

The Benefits of Being Debt-Free and Liquid

1. Having your own money—cash that does not come from an investor—forces you to budget within your means.
2. Your decision-making is based on your true needs and not your debt.
3. Cash is king and ensures that you will never be forced to liquidate assets or take out loans to pay vendors.
4. Having your own ensures that you will not have to answer to anyone or compromise yourself in any way.
5. You can say no anytime you want, and you don't have to take another's objectives into consideration.

No matter how profitable a quarter you have, set a little aside and put it in the bank. It gives you peace of mind and allows you to enjoy the full benefit of a payoff when you do succeed.

deal with a big-box retailer requires taking out loans or losing equity to an outside investor in exchange for a much-needed injection of cash. They lose the entrepreneurial spirit and effectively become employees of their new owners. But we choose to grow organically, investing in our staff through additional training, full benefits, and profit sharing as we continue to forge mutually beneficial relationships with select distributors and makers.

We are always looking for the right partners, who share our values and understand the heart and soul of Miss Jessie's. While there are sharks that can hurt you, there also are dolphins that can lift you up and help you. These more benign investors offer four things: cash to grow your business; expertise in mass retail; introductions and access to distributors and retailers; and money for your own pocket. Successful small-business owners are continually reinvesting all their worth in the growth of the business and never their own bank accounts.

The financial relief provided by an investor can be tempting. However, we were able to resist because we were debt-free and had huge savings. We continue to hope that, ultimately, we will find that perfect combination of mentor and investor who can stand beside us in the years to come. But expansion isn't something we need for its own sake. That's why, when the offer isn't right on all fronts, we can afford to say no. If we have to sit out a dance or two, we do. Bigger isn't better; better is better.

A HUMAN ENTERPRISE

★

Our evolution as a business is about much more than a higher sales volume. It concerns how we are growing as people and how we act within the community that's supported us from the beginning. This is important, because a brand isn't just some label you stick on a great product. In many ways, it represents your values, as well as the aspirations and beliefs of the customers you serve. A business, particularly one that makes products dedicated to enhancing the lives of others in some way, needs to show its humanity. Besides, there is so much more to being successful than financial rewards. It has to mean something.

For Madam C. J. Walker, her business became a platform to give back. She became a champion for civil rights, education, and empowering women and children in underserved communities across America. We have been taking steps to help others through scholarships, donating to community groups and boys' and girls' clubs. Whether it's speaking with a group of high school girls or giving away our orange Miss Jessie's gift bags full of product samples like Leave-In Condish and Pillow Soft Curls, to help out young girls and single working mothers, or offering free tips on hair, we are reaching back to groups of people with whom we identify.

We aspire to be a brand with a heartbeat, and being a helpful part of the community is part of being complete. Beyond our knowledge of curly hair, we have many other jewels to share, and we understand the rule of reciprocity: Sharing and giving are going to benefit everyone, including us. Finding ways to be good to people gives us immense satisfaction. Helping people or friends find their own independence, or even offering stable jobs to hardworking individuals, makes us feel whole.

When we contract out our work, we try as often as we can to partner with other small businesses and individuals, whether they are PR firms, makeup artists, production teams, or other hairstylists. We look at these young men and women who are striving and see ourselves. We take a chance on them because people like Joseph, my first hairstyling employer, or Sonia Alleyne, editor of the former *Black Elegance* magazine, who helped us get our first advertising campaign, took a chance on us.

We also reach back to our old friends and hire them for various projects. We nurture and develop our employees, giving them full benefits. It is important that when you ask your staff to work hard—and we do—that you are willing to reward their hard work. Treating your staff fairly is not only the proper thing to do; it is also simply good business. You can avoid high turnover rates and the cost in time, energy, and money that it takes to train new staff. Over time, you will have and maintain a loyal and experienced team to support you and your business. We spot their talent and promote from within. My personal assistant, for example, has worked in every department, moving up from packing boxes to helping supervise the salon floor, to executing my ideas on video and photo shoots, writing out scripts, hiring models, setting up catering, and generally fulfilling his dream of getting into video production. It helps us, because he knows how exacting I am and knows how to meet my expectations, which means I don't have to outsource the job to a video director. By grooming him for this spot, I now have a loyal employee who appreciates the opportunity to stretch himself.

This is what giving back looks like for us. Whether it's a

small favor or a gesture, being able to help and support our community opens up our whole world on so many levels. It's what our namesake, Miss Jessie, was all about. She never preached. Instead, she showed us what love is through countless small acts of kindness. Miss Jessie didn't just teach us about independence, resourcefulness, and creativity at her kitchen table. She showed us her humanity and integrity simply by doing.

We give back because we are extremely grateful. Although we didn't have anything handed to us, we had a solid foundation on which to build. Our father, Jimmy Branch, taught us a great deal that we have carried forward to this day.

We don't know what the future holds for us. Our story is still unfolding. Like all great enterprises, we are a business with a beating heart. Miss Jessie's is a living thing, constantly changing and evolving. But whatever happens, that change will continue to be on our own terms. The time-tested recipe that makes Miss Jessie's a truly authentic brand will remain intact, as will the single most important ingredient of everything we produce—love.

Epilogue

★ ★ ★

MISS JESSIE'S EIGHT KEY INGREDIENTS

★

Common Sense

Follow your gut. You know when it's wrong or right for you, so filter out the noise and listen to your inner voice. That first instinct is almost always correct. It doesn't mean you shouldn't stretch or try something new, but common sense should always prevail, no matter what the experts say.

Choose Your People Wisely

Know your partners, including those you work with. We use the interviewing and negotiating process to evaluate who is the right fit for us. At the end of the day, it's about chemistry. You have to like, trust, and respect the people you are working with on a regular basis. Something good will always come out of a positive relationship.

Reciprocity

Foster mutual respect. There needs to be an organizational hierarchy, because someone must be accountable. But respect goes both ways. Employees will give you their best work when they know it's appreciated, and that you believe in them. Expect much; motivate more.

Business Karma

Be fair. Treat others the way you would want to be treated, in all things. This includes competition, business partners, contractors, associates, and employees. Whether it's making sure people get their money on time, or shipping out product well ahead of a deadline, people remember when you've been professional and courteous. You will always be first in line.

Manage Expectations

Have clarity from beginning to end. Whether it's with family members who work with you or employees, clear communication about roles and expectations will save you a lot of pain. Let others know what is expected, and listen in turn to understand their goals and concerns. When everyone is on the same page, things flow and business is more productive.

Live Within Your Means

Trim the fat whenever necessary. There is no reason to run your business or your life beyond your means. Even when we made those huge sales numbers with Target, Titi and I never paid ourselves more than low six figures. Work with the budget you have, and when you have a good year, bank it. This will ensure liquidity and security when the unforeseen happens.

Don't Be Greedy

Greed is not good. It can cloud your judgment. You will make bad deals if you are focused only on money. Remind yourself why you chose the business you are in. It's usually because you have a passion for something and the money is secondary. Keep it that way.

Never Rest on Your Laurels

Constantly reevaluate. Nothing stands still. As situations change, you and your business need to change. Life and business are about continually adapting to the reality on the ground. When Miss Jessie realized that the situation in her childhood home down south was becoming untenable, she did not hesitate to pull up stakes and start a new life in Poughkeepsie. She kept it moving, and her life was richer and more fulfilling as a result.

A LIFETIME OF LEARNING

★

I'd like to think that, over the years, we've learned a few things and developed some core principles. From the time we were teenagers living under our father's roof, Titi and I have been businesswomen. All told, we ran five different enterprises. They were:

★ The Branch Cleaning Agency
★ A one-chair salon that grew into Curve on Bond Street

* The curly-hair specialist salon in Bed-Stuy, which became Miss Jessie's salon, now on Broadway in Manhattan
* Miss Jessie's, the underground e-commerce business that sold product from our basement
* Miss Jessie's, the global, mass retail brand

Each of these ventures gave us a wealth of knowledge about how to start, grow, expand, and evolve a business, whether in the service sector or the mass consumer market. But there is a reason why our core principles are as much about values as they are about business strategy. Business is a fundamentally human activity. It reflects our humanity. That's why, of all our business principles, the most important one is "Be true to yourself." Never step away from those values you were raised with, and keep being you. It's taken you this far, and it can take you all the way.

LETTER TO TITI

★ ★ ★

Dearest Titi,

When I think back on our lives together, my heart is full with gratitude. When no one else believed in me, you always did. You stood beside me, pushing me to take it to another level even before I knew I wanted to do more. You carried so much of the load, enabling me, helping me to execute my vision, and sharing in all the tasks necessary to keep us moving forward. We could not have built Miss Jessie's at the same speed or with the same level of satisfaction, if we had not been working side by side. You were an essential part of the recipe that made it so incredibly good. Without you, the adventure would not have been nearly as sweet.

You've been my partner in crime since the day I was born. We did everything together, and growing up with you as my protector and best friend gave me the security of knowing that I would always be unconditionally loved. Throughout the years you have been my greatest teacher. You encouraged me and made me bold, all the while setting aside your own personal needs to see me thrive. You amazed me with your creativity and willingness to try anything to come up with our winning formula. You, like Miss Jessie, were a mother of invention, and I look back on your many accomplishments with awe and pride.

Above all you were a devoted coparent to Faison. You helped me raise him as if he were your own. You were so much more than "Aunt Titi." You cared for him as any mother would love her firstborn, and my son flourished with the extra dose of maternal love you gave him. You nurtured me, too.

Yes, we had our conflicts, as sisters often do. Our bond was as strong as our expectations of each other were high. But, for all our ups and downs, I feel an intense and abiding love for you—my big sister. In many ways, we raised each other, and knowing we had each other's backs gave us an inner strength and confidence that took us farther than we ever thought possible.

Your rare beauty, generosity, and compassion will be sorely missed. Your curiosity and intelligence, the way you always extended yourself to others with countless acts of kindness and words of inspiration will never be forgotten. Titi, you were among the brightest lights in the room, always ready to laugh and engage. Your rich voice commanded attention and respect, and you moved through the world with such elegance and composure. You turned heads with those bright eyes, that magnetic smile, and that gorgeous head of blond, brown, black, and gold curls—a fitting crown for my queen.

Although you left us far too soon, I am blessed to have been given the chance to spend more than forty years standing shoulder to shoulder with you. I hope and pray that you have been reunited with our beloved grandmother in heaven. May Miss Jessie fold you inside her warm embrace. May she love and care for you the way you loved and cared for us.

Rest in peace, my darling big sister, and know that because of all the wisdom you shared with me I will run this business as your legacy, implementing your principles and ideas with emphasis on your grace, warmth, and style. *Miss Jessie's* will be my tribute to your memory, and I will live to make you proud.

Your ever-loving,
Miko

ACKNOWLEDGMENTS

★ ★ ★

There are so many positive influences in my life for whom I am grateful—people who shaped me as an entrepreneur, a woman, and a mother. My whole adult life has been about living beyond my father's expectations, to show him that I *am* smart; I *am* qualified. Jimmy Branch, Dad, has been my driving force, my unlikely inspiration to succeed. Every step I take, every decision I make, the same questions echo in my mind: *WWDD— what would Daddy do?* and *WWDT—what would Daddy think?* Thank you to my father for being an amazing teacher and devoted parent. Daddy, you taught me so much about life, parenting, and business. I am thankful to have been exposed to such a wonderful man.

Titi, thank you for being my big sister, friend, supporter, partner, coparent, and protector. I have learned so much from you in all situations, good and bad. I am truly thankful to have spent much of my life with you.

Above all, I want to thank my son. Miss Jessie's would not exist if it were not for Faison Branch. Period. We could not have transformed an industry and inspired many to embrace their natural selves had he not been born. My son made a woman out of me. Faison, you are my greatest inspiration and motivator to be the best Miko I can be.

I am eternally grateful to my late grandmother, Jessie Mae Branch. She is my ultimate example of strength, dignity, independence, respect, pride, family, and love. In many respects, I *am* Miss Jessie. Everyone in my family says that!

To our mother, Karen Akemi Matsumoto, thank you for being my mom. You introduced me to art and beauty from an early age. I am forever grateful and thankful for your love and contribution to my greatest love, my son. Thank you for helping me to raise my king.

To our customers and clients: The loyalty and support you have given me has been tremendous. Without that, we could not have realized so many of my dreams, and we are eternally grateful.

To our business partners: we've been fortunate to do business with many kind and fair people. These partnerships have helped to propel our companies forward. We are truly thankful.

To our employees: we could not have done this without you and we are thankful to you.

To my friends, you know who you are! I deeply appreciate how you have been there for me, accepting me as I am. I feel blessed to be able to spend time with such wonderful, loving, and supportive friends.

To my extended family: Uncle Irvin, Aunt Hilda, Aunt Lorraine, Uncle Ricardo, and all my cousins, aunts, and uncles. You have been cheering me on while always keeping it real with me, and for that I am thankful.

I'd also like to thank the amazing team on this book project: Tracy Sherrod, Samantha Marshall, and Reeves Carter for being supportive, smart, skillful, insightful, professional, caring, and patient while putting this project together and helping me to realize my dream to tell our story. Thank you also to our dedicated literary agents, Carol Mann and Madeleine Morel.

Last but not least, I thank God. I thank Him for giving me the knowledge, wisdom, and understanding to navigate this amazing life. He has been there for me all along, and I am so very humbled and grateful. I know I am truly blessed.

GLOSSARY OF RETAIL TERMS

★ ★ ★

Ad dollars—Money spent on advertising.

Assortments—Can mean a few things: the collection of items within a brand, or the total collection of items in a planogram, or other collections of items.

Broker—The liaison between manufacturer and retailer. A broker decodes the process and practices of the retailer, thereby making it easier for the manufacturer to do business with the retailer. The manufacturer pays the broker.

Brand blocking—Placing all items from a brand together rather than blocking by segment. For instance, all shampoos together, then all conditioners, stylers, and so on. This is in contrast to putting together all products from one brand. Consumers most often shop by brands they are loyal to in categories; they shop by segment if they don't care what they buy and are motivated only by price, size, or other factors.

Buybacks—Products that are returned to the manufacturer for various reasons. The manufacturer refunds the large retailer for the value. Most common for outdated or discontinued merchandise.

Charge-backs—Deductions taken from payment to a vendor for any number of things—compliance charges, defectives, scans, etc.

Collect—Often referred to as FOB (free on board) the vendor's warehouse, meaning the vendor is responsible for the cost of getting the goods to their warehouse and the retailer takes over from there.

Comp shop—Discovering a lower price from a competitor and matching it.

Distributor—Normally buys the product from the manufacturer and resells to the retailer. Most likely seen with smaller brands that want a presence in larger chains or channels of distribution.

Drop ship—Generally shipping directly to stores, or in some cases, direct to the consumer.

End cap—A display on the front or back of an aisle; may rotate regularly.

FDM—Food, drug, mass. Food: grocery (Kroger, Safeway, Publix); drug (Walgreens, CVS, Rite Aid); mass (Target, Walmart).

Forecasting—Predicting the level of orders or sales by day, week, month, quarter, year, or longer.

Funding for discounts or specials at food, drug, or mass retailers—Normally, promotions are funded at full retail, in which the manufacturer has responsibility for the promotion and the retailer has no out-of-pocket expenses. If funded at cost, the retailer is investing the margin difference between cost and full retail.

In-line—What is contained in the aisle and generally updates only once or sometimes twice a year.

IRI/Nielsen numbers (tracking sales) —Sales data (each time an item scans) that is sold by mass retailers to IRI and Nielsen, which then formats and resells the data to manufacturers and others. Allows a look at competitive sales.

Margins —Net profit margin percentage equals net profit (retail minus cost) divided by the retail.

Markdowns—Multiple meanings: 1) reduction in retail to clear product out of the store; 2) advertising scans; 3) reduction in retail to match other retailers; 4) reduction of defectives.

Planogram —The "map" of products placed on the shelf. Very specifically defined by location, then item, number of facings, and number of items per facing.

Price points—Retail prices.

Shrinkage—Theft by shoppers or employees. Normally discovered as a discrepancy between physical inventory and what the system shows should be on hand.

Rollbacks—Walmart's approach to pricing discounts.

Shipping—Prepaid (vendor includes the cost of shipping in their cost) or collect (where the retailer picks up the goods in exchange for a lower cost).

SKU—Stock keeping unit. Each individual item is an SKU.

Store counts—Number of stores a retailer has, most often broken down by region, demographics, or distribution.

Suggested retail pricing—Avoids antitrust violations. Retailers cannot conspire to keep prices at certain levels. Some retailers will allow MAP (minimum advertised price) pricing, but it gets iffy regarding antitrust.

TPCs—Temporary price cuts (Target).

TPRs—Temporary price reductions (other retailers).

THE LANGUAGE OF HAIR: DEFINITIONS

★ ★ ★

Afro—A thick hairstyle with very tight curls that stick out all around the head.

Bantu Knots—When hair is sectioned off in diamond, triangle, or square shapes and twisted into knots.

Braid Out—A styling method where three pieces of hair are interlaced.

Braids—Woven pattern created in hair with origins from Africa.

Double Process Color—Two steps: The hair is bleached to remove natural or colored hair pigments; a new color is then added into the hair to create the desired shade.

Double Strand Twist—A styling method where two pieces of hair are twisted together.

Dry Twist—Hair is blown out and Double-Strand-Twisted.

European Styles—Referring mostly to straight styles.

Kitchen—Back area of the hair that tends to be more coarse/tightly coiled, sensitive, or fragile.

Locs—Matted coils of hair.

Mineral oil—A distillation product of petroleum, especially one used as a moisturizer.

Natural—Not chemically processed; God-given.

No Animal Testing—Products or chemicals are not tested on animals.

Parabens—Preservatives that are used to increase shelf life of products.

Protective Styling—Styling the hair in a way that prevents damage from everyday elements.

Relaxed—Hair that is chemically altered to be straight.

Shrinkage—When your hair shrivels up.

Stretch Out—Maximizing the length of one's hair by blow-drying, twisting, or braiding.

Shingling—Smoothing hair down between two fingers, a small section at a time, for maximum definition. Method created by Titi Branch.

Silkener—A chemical process in which the hair texture is chemically altered to create a looser, shinier, more defined, and manageable hair pattern.

Single-Process Color—A new color or toner is applied all over to create a new base color. The hair is lifted and deposited in one easy step.

Sulfates—Cleaning ingredients that are added to products to make them clean using suds.

Textures

　Coily—Very circular wound curls.

　Kinky—A torsion twist where the hair strand turns around itself.

　Curls—A spiral or wave.

　Nappy—A negative reference to tightly coiled hair in its natural state.

　TWA—Tween weeny Afro.

　Wet Twists—Hair is wet and Double-Strand-Twisted.

PRODUCT DEFINITIONS

★ ★ ★

From Lightest to Heaviest

TRANSITIONER'S MAGIC

★ Brings texture to straight hair while moisturizing your new natural growth as well as reviving and coating your relaxed hair
★ Excellent for transitioning from relaxed to natural hair
★ Fights frizz and prevents hair shrinkage
★ Provides super-soft hold, natural shine, and needed moisture
★ Enhanced with soybean and avocado
★ Great wash-and-go styler and rod set
★ Lightest hold

MULTICULTURAL CURLS

★ Wash-and-go styler, targeting multi-textured and multi-ethnic curls.
★ Soft and lightweight.
★ Enhanced with safflower oil and olive fruit oil.

★ Gives your curls uniformity and manageability while fighting frizz and adding just the right amount of super-soft hold.

★ Lighter hold.

PILLOW SOFT CURLS

★ Fuller lightweight hold.

★ Provides a soft, fluffy, big, softly defined curl pattern.

★ Innovative technology combines fabricare with hair care by providing antistatic technology.

★ Great wash-and-go styler for wavy, curly, tight-curly, and transitioners hair.

QUICK CURLS

★ Universal to all curly, kinky, and wavy hair textures.

★ Lightweight to medium hold.

★ Creates curl definition.

★ Will help cut down frizz.

★ Wash-and-go styling lotion.

JELLY SOFT CURLS

★ Medium hold/soft gel.

★ Crunch-free gel that aids in creating medium definition.

★ Great styler for wash-and-go on wavy, curly, tight-curly.

★ Great styler for two-strand twists and coils for kinky hair.

★ Great styler for rod sets on transitioners hair.

★ Fast-drying.

COILY CUSTARD

★ Wash-and-go styler, targeting kinky or coily hair.

★ Transforms tight, frizzy 'fros to loose, moisturized curls.

★ Nongreasy with major shine.

★ Enhanced with agave and coconut oil.

★ Slippery texture coats each frizzy strand with a dose of moisture and shine that enhances curl pattern, reduces frizz, and fights curl shrinkage.

STRETCH SILKENING CRÈME

★ Medium weight/medium hold.

★ First in the series of "heavier" crèmes for Miss Jessie's stylers.

★ Excellent shine factor.

★ Great for wash-and-go for curly and tight-curly.

★ Great for two-strand twists for kinky.

★ Great for rod sets for transitioners.

CURLY MERINGUE

★ Medium-firm hold.

★ Second-heaviest crème in Miss Jessie's collection.

★ Medium-hold factor boosts curl formation.

★ Excellent styler for wash-and-go for curly, tight-curly.

★ Excellent styler for rod setting for transitoners.

★ Satin shine.

CURLY PUDDING

★ Firm hold/extra shine.
★ Richest, heaviest crème-based styler in the collection.
★ Firmest hold for long-lasting curls.
★ Great for "ramen noodle" definition.
★ Great shine factor.
★ Excellent for tight-curly wash-and-go.
★ Excellent for twist sets, rod sets, or coils for kinky and transitioner textures.

SUPER SLIP SUDSY SHAMPOO

★ Great detangling/moisturizing shampoo designed for effective cleansing and encouraging a clean, smooth surface for application of styling products.
★ Preps the hair for the proper product application to encourage a smooth curl.
★ Gentle enough for three-times-a-week use.
★ Best for any hair type in need of a slippery sudsing shampoo.
★ Contains sulfates.

CRÈME DE LA CURL/CO-WASH

★ No-lather, sulfate-free formula.
★ Removes product buildup and washes away the daily grime without leaving your hair or scalp dried out.
★ Suds-free cleaning, hydration, and moisturizing elements help the hair and scalp maintain a healthy luster.

CRÈME DE LA CREME

★ Luxurious lightweight conditioner excellent for wavy or curly hair in need of some smoothing.

★ Not heavy or deeply moisturizing but effective enough to provide a smooth surface for product application.

★ Great for waves and curls in need of light conditioning and smoothing.

★ Does not weigh hair down.

★ Great for fine-textured hair.

★ Great daily conditioner.

LEAVE-IN CONDISH

★ A lightweight moisturizing styling "prep" for your curls.

★ Detangler that acts as the ultimate frizz fighter.

★ Enhanced with soybean and aloe, locking in an extra layer of moisture.

★ Coats and protects curls as you style.

SUPER SWEETBACK TREATMENT

★ Intensive reparative treatment for dry, flyaway curly hair.

★ Rich moisturizing treatment that aids in the ultimate smoothing.

★ Contains centella extract, a growth treatment to aid in growing out curly hair.

★ Excellent for tight-curly, kinky, and transitioners hair types.

★ Essential prep for making curls soft, supple, and easy to position.

RAPID RECOVERY TREATMENT

★ Intensive reparative treatment for dry, flyaway curly hair.
★ Rich moisturizing treatment that aids in ultimate smoothing.
★ Excellent treatment for color-treated, dry, damaged hair.
★ Excellent for damaged wavy, damaged curly, tight-curly, kinky, and transitioners hair types.
★ Essential prep for making curls soft, supple, and easy to position.

BABY BUTTERCREME

★ Superb moisturizing capabilities.
★ Makes dried knotty hair more manageable.
★ Gives a natural sheen to hair.
★ Softens dry textures.
★ Provides a moist, soft texture, making hair touchable.
★ Great for kids' grooming.
★ Great daily maintenance for tight-curly and kinky hair.

CURLY BUTTERCREME

★ Superb moisturizer.
★ Tingling scalp sensation.
★ Gives a natural sheen to hair.
★ Softens dry textures.
★ Provides a moist, soft texture, making hair touchable.
★ Great daily maintenance for tight-curly and kinky hair.

ABOUT THE AUTHOR

★ ★ ★

MIKO BRANCH is the co-founder and CEO of Miss Jessie's LLC. She is celebrated for transforming the hair-care industry by pioneering an entirely new category of products specifically for natural and curly hair. She was featured in *Women's Wear Daily*, appeared on the cover of *Beauty Inc.* as a trailblazer, and *Ebony* listed her as one of its Power 100 Innovators and Influencers. She has also been honored by New York University and Delta Sigma Theta for her entrepreneurship. Miss Jessie's award-winning products have been featured in *O, the Oprah Magazine*, *Teen Vogue*, *Redbook*, *Essence*, *Allure*, *Latina*, and other publications. She lives in New York with her son.

Chicagos dog lady - 1940
Violar Larson farved
Home Cemday

Wind Blew Inn - flapper -

Adam Selser 312-981-7200

Rebecca Robeson - Robeson Design

Loom Knitting

Tax Lien
Tax Deed Sales
Private Lender - foreclosure
Code Violations, Tax Defaults
How Do Buy a house with a Tax Lien
If you Pay Back taxes Do you own it

Buy a foreclosure direct
from a courthouse

"foreclosure Investor"
Equity on
Property

Cash Buyers List

Judicial foreclosure
stopping or vacating foreclosure

Did the notary Republic
Actually witness signing

Casefile-Docet#   master
                         morgage

Title Search into a lawyer

property title vs property deed
Deed of Reconveyance
Action in Lieu of
    Prerogative writs

Backpage.com
eBay classifieds.com

Get Deed Take Over Homes
    in foreclosure

Jimmy Lee,

make Sure your with someone
who is worth it

Have the Clarity to understand
and who is worthy of us
(walking thirty them
Certain de vistation
and when its Time to walk
away. Not everybody you love
is meant to be the person
you build a life with

Kickboxing
Dance fitness

Always have Common Sense

make it your mission
    to teach about Love, wisdom

never depend on any one
    be independant

Opportunity is everywhere

navy conducting
testing